MAXIMIZING '*IT*' VALUE

Through Operational Excellence

*A Definitive Guide to
Twelve Best Practices in
Applications Support
and Maintenance*

Dr. Peter M. Thompson

Includes a Reprint
of the HBR Article:
"IT Doesn't Matter"
by Nicholas G. Carr

"IT Doesn't Matter" by Nicholas G. Carr & "Does IT Matter? An HBR Debate" © 2003 by *Harvard Business Review*, reprinted by permission

Note for Librarians: A cataloguing record for this book is available from Library and Archives Canada at www.collectionscanada.ca/amicus/index-e.html
ISBN 1-4120-7289-1

Printed in Victoria, BC, Canada. Printed on paper with minimum 30% recycled fibre. Trafford's print shop runs on "green energy" from solar, wind and other environmentally-friendly power sources.
Published by RIS, Inc.
www.risglobal.com

Offices in Canada, USA, Ireland and UK
This book was published *on-demand* in cooperation with Trafford Publishing. On-demand publishing is a unique process and service of making a book available for retail sale to the public taking advantage of on-demand manufacturing and Internet marketing. On-demand publishing includes promotions, retail sales, manufacturing, order fulfilment, accounting and collecting royalties on behalf of the author.

Book sales for North America and international:
Trafford Publishing, 6E–2333 Government St.,
Victoria, BC V8T 4P4 CANADA
phone 250 383 6864 (toll-free 1 888 232 4444)
fax 250 383 6804; email to orders@trafford.com
Book sales in Europe:
Trafford Publishing (UK) Limited, 9 Park End Street, 2nd Floor
Oxford, UK OX1 1HH UNITED KINGDOM
phone 44 (0)1865 722 113 (local rate 0845 230 9601)
facsimile 44 (0)1865 722 868; info.uk@trafford.com
Order online at:
trafford.com/05-2184

10 9 8

TABLE OF CONTENTS

Appendices.

TABLES AND FIGURES

Preface

In his landmark article "IT Doesn't Matter," Nicholas G. Carr begins by describing an IT trend-line that cannot continue. IT as a percentage of capital expenditures, according to the U.S. Department of Commerce's Bureau of Economic Analysis, rises from five percent in 1965 to fifteen percent in the early '80s to thirty percent in the '90s—and to almost fifty percent today. During the same time period, global IT expenditures have grown to almost $3 trillion. The wakeup call in Carr's article is that this type of IT growth cannot continue forever. Something must change.

Carr predicts that the great IT build-out is near completion. Using railways and electric power grids as historical metaphors, Carr asserts that IT is quickly becoming an ubiquitous commodity that in itself has no competitive advantage. Like any other asset, he claims, the competitive advantage in IT will become operational excellence, not the fact that you acquired/created the commodity first

If Carr's prediction is right, the implications for the IT profession are truly profound. A fundamental shift in the way of thinking within the whole IT community will be required: a move away from the current glorious project/technology "change the world" way of thinking, to a more mundane application/process "manage what we have" way of thinking. In other words, corporate IT professionals of the future will not be working on new projects using new technology. Instead, they will be maintaining and enhancing existing applications by following a well defined applications support, maintenance, and enhancement process. Applications Development programmers will work mostly in university labs and software development companies. Only Applications Support and Maintenance programmers will be required at a typical corporation.

A quick tour of any bookstore demonstrates the immensity of this change. Whole sections of books are devoted to explaining the latest technology and how to build or manage software development in these technologies. IT courses, magazines, certifications, and interest groups are all oriented to new development projects. When it comes to managing and maintaining existing applications, information is scarce and hard to find.

From a corporate perspective, the change is also immense. Treacy and Wiersema[1], in their best-selling book, *The Discipline of Market Leaders*, state that an organization must choose one of three value disciplines as its underlying operating model: Product Leadership, Customer Intimacy, or Operational Excellence. While a capability in all three is important, one must be the primary value discipline to drive decisions, resolve conflicts, and set priorities. In pre-Carr IT organizations, one of Product Leadership (creativity and innovation) or Customer Intimacy (give the users what they want) was the accepted norm. If IT truly is a commodity, as Carr believes, then Operational Excellence becomes the primary value discipline to drive IT decisions. This change is truly revolutionary and has enormous implications throughout the corporation.

The changes are most significant for the CIO. Carr's new rules with respect to the IT management are: (i) spend less, (ii) follow, don't lead, and (iii) focus on vulnerabilities, not opportunities. These rules, combined with IT's Operational Excellence value discipline, mean that corporations no longer need or want CIO's who are experts in project management or technology. Instead, they need business-minded operational experts who can enhance value to the business by leveraging the installed base of computer applications, turning them into useful, reliable, low-cost assets.

From a shareholder perspective, the change means IT staff will now be

---

1   Treacy and Wiersema, *The Discipline of Market Leaders*, published 1995.

viewed primarily as custodians of existing wealth (managing existing computer applications) as opposed to creators of new wealth (building new computer applications). Furthermore, IT will be expected to integrate into the corporation and follow normal business practices—managing computer applications as corporate assets and following normal "plan, execute, report" business cycles.

Is Carr's prediction right? Will applications development disappear entirely from the corporate landscape? This is perhaps a bit extreme. For most companies, Applications Support and Maintenance (ASM) and the associated operational excellence way of thinking will become the primary role of IT. Applications Development (AD) will continue to exist but will take on a research and development (R&D) type role outside normal business operations.

To enable operational excellence, IT must become a suite of IT Application Service Chains (shown in figure A). An IT Application Service Chain is an information-service orientated derivative of the Value Chain developed by Porter[2] in 1980. Each IT Application Service Chain links to a profit center – viewed as either a Value Chain, or in the case of services, the Corporate Service Chain (shown in figure B). Application developers, in their R&D role, are not a part of the IT Application Service Chain. Instead they are like supply chain managers, expected to use standard, off-the-shelf, low-cost software/hardware components to create and improve the IT Application Service Chain. In other words, application developers will be sophisticated business people able to buy/build links in the IT Application Service Chain to enable a better overall service to the end consumer.

---

2   Michael Porter, Competitive Advantage, published 1980

FIGURE A. IT APPLICATION SERVICE CHAIN

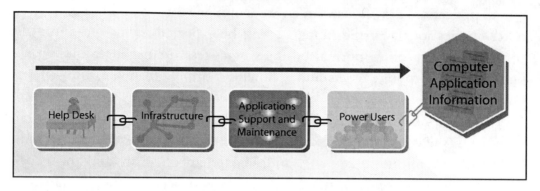

FIGURE B. CORPORATE SERVICE CHAIN

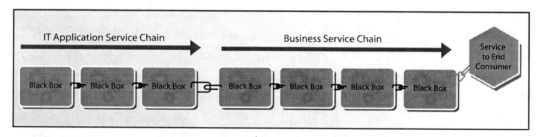

This book, "*Maximizing IT Value through Operational Excellence*" takes Carr's premise that IT is a commodity and argues that this means the appropriate value discipline for IT is Operational Excellence. Operational excellence requires, by definition:

i)   A common set of best practices that can be centrally managed and rigorously followed.

ii) A suite of metrics that can measure the effectiveness of best practices and enable predictability in "if we do this, we will get that".

Hence, the title extension in this book of "*A Definitive Guide to Twelve Best Practices in Applications Support and Maintenance*". These twelve best practices are methods, techniques, and processes that have existed in the heads of ASM veterans for years, but that have never been written down and published. Instead, they have been passed down verbally from generation to generation using anecdotes and the good old school of "watch me carefully, then you do it". Having been an IT professional and ASM practitioner for thirty years, I thought it time to share these best practices publicly.

As a final note, it should be recognized that the concept of operational excellence is not entirely new and untried in IT. In fact, the results of introducing operational excellence into IT can be truly astounding. As described in Carr's article, a study by Alinean Corporation showed companies delivering highest economic returns spend 0.8 percent of revenue on IT, versus an industry average of 3.7 percent of revenue. This is not just a simple budget-cutting exercise. As Alinean CEO Tom Pisello points out in a letter of response (see Afterword), the worst-performing companies also spend 0.8 percent of revenue on IT. The study showed no correlation between IT spending and financial performance. That said, for leading companies who can add three per cent of revenue to the bottom line via operational excellence in IT, there is a whopping competitive advantage!

Chapter 1

APPLICATIONS SUPPORT AND MAINTENANCE: THE NEW IT DISCIPLINE

Approximately $3 trillion is spent annually on IT, of that, about $1 trillion is spent on Applications Support and Maintenance (ASM)[3]. Despite its huge cost, ASM—the activity of supporting, maintaining, and enhancing existing computer applications—has remained largely ignored and "unmanaged" by IT. Instead, there has been a fifty-year focus on new applications development using the latest technology, in what Nicholas G. Carr calls the great IT buildout. As Carr states in his article "IT Doesn't Matter," (see Afterword) corporate IT strategy has been driven by vendor pressures, where new hardware and software opportunities absorb all the management focus and attention. The result is a huge installed base of computer applications that are not being properly managed or leveraged.

This imbalance is about to change. Carr predicts that going forward, large investments in applications development (AD) with the idea of gaining a competitive advantage will end. He claims that IT is now a commodity-driven environment, where any IT-related competitive edge, developed at huge human and capital cost to an organization, can be quickly replicated by a competitor at a fraction of the cost. Furthermore, an early developer using new technology risks missing an evolving IT standard, thereby incurring additional costs

---

3   This is based on the assumption that a typical company spends about 40% of their IT budget on Infrastructure, 30% on Applications Support and Maintenance (ASM), and 30% on Applications Development (AD).

not incurred by competitors for converting to the new standard. This points to an IT environment where competitive advantage with respect to IT will no longer be in application development (AD). Instead, the competitive advantage will be operational excellence in applications support and maintenance (ASM)—knowing how to leverage the installed base of computer applications with minimal cost. It is a discipline that traditionally has been unrecognized and undervalued in IT. Hence… Applications Support and Maintenance: The New IT Discipline.

IT Discipline – explained

A discipline is defined by three components:

i)   the methodology, a set of rules to follow,

ii) the tools needed to follow the methodology and accomplish the task, and

iii) the people trained and certified in the use of the methodology and tools.

The following table describes the familiar disciplines of medicine, engineering, and carpentry.

TABLE 1. DISCIPLINE TABLE FOR MEDICINE, ENGINEERING, AND CARPENTRY

	Medicine	Engineering	Carpentry
Methodology	CPS (Compendium of Pharmaceuticals and Specialties) produced annually and used extensively by medical professionals when prescribing drugs	Standard Handbook for Civil Engineers (Handbook)	Knowledge that houses are framed using a sole plate, double top plates, and 16- inch centered studs.
Tools	Stethoscope, blood pressure gauge, tongue depressor	Calculator (slide ruler), draftsman's T-square and triangle.	Circular saw, carpenter square, measuring tape, hammer.
Certification	Canadian Medical Association	Association of Professional Engineers	Apprentice, Journeyman, Master

Closer examination of this table shows these descriptions to be definitions of sub-disciplines within the overall discipline. The methodology and tools described for medicine are found in a family doctor's office, not in the hospital operating room of a brain surgeon. The engineering description defines the methodology and tools for civil engineering, not mechanical or electrical engineering. In carpentry, the definition is for a house framer, not a cabinet-maker.

Just as engineering has evolved into different sub-disciplines (electrical, mechanical, chemical), as has medicine (urology, dermatology, ophthalmology), so too is IT evolving—although some fail to recognize this truth. Help desk, infrastructure, ASM, and AD are all different and distinct sub-disciplines, each with their own unique methodology, tools, best practices, training, and certification. Corporate executives and the public at large must learn to understand these IT sub-disciplines and utilize them accordingly. Just as you would not ask a urologist about a skin problem or an electrical engineer to build a bridge, you should not ask AD staff to maintain existing applications or infrastructure specialists to develop new applications. Each IT problem/opportunity requires a focus into a separate sub-discipline capability within IT. For example, the inability to align IT to the business (a chronic problem with IT) is a symptom that the wrong IT sub-discipline is being asked to do the wrong thing—like a pediatrician struggling to do surgery. An IT applications development group will quickly align within a project-oriented environment, but will struggle to align with a business operations manager who is providing a day-to-day service.

Traditionally, all of IT has been viewed primarily as an application development (AD) discipline; a sequence of big new technology projects designed to enhance the corporation's competitiveness in large, discrete steps. We are now saying that IT must be viewed primarily as an ASM discipline, where IT becomes not a series of projects to be managed by project managers, but rather a suite of processes to be managed by process managers…a new and different IT discipline.

Applications Support and Maintenance (ASM) – defined

What is ASM? ASM is a process! It is a process around sustaining and leveraging computer application assets. ASM does not own, nor is it responsible for, the computer applications. The line of business owns and is responsible for them. ASM is the custodian of the applications. It is charged with providing services that keep the applications reliable, useful, and low-cost.

So long as application integrity is preserved, ASM, in its custodial role, is not in itself of high strategic value to the corporation and does not require extensive business knowledge. This differs from AD. Where ASM's responsibility is to provide reliable, useful, and low-cost applications, AD's responsibility is to have the business and technology vision to create new wealth. In AD, new applications are being designed and new technology is being applied to radically change the look and feel of a product or service. Clearly, AD is of very high strategic value and requires extensive business knowledge. The diagram in figure 1 explains these concepts by showing how the Application Service Chain feeds into Porter's Corporate Value Chain. Value Chain functions are strategic and need extensive business knowledge. Application Service

Chain functions are operational and require less business knowledge.

Figure 1. Strategic Value vs Business Knowledge Requirements

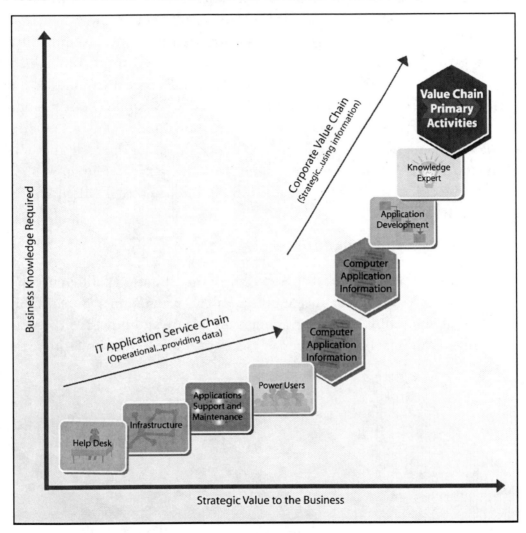

The application itself is of course both strategic and operational—strategic in that it is an integral part of the corporate vision of the future, and operational in that computer applications often contain much of the information, business rules, and knowledge needed to operate a line of business.

In IT and the public in general, there is often fuzziness around differentiating Applications Support and Maintenance (ASM) from Applications Development (AD). Some people view these two distinct disciplines as one entity called Application Management. Others use ASM and AD interchangeably, whichever suits their fancy. Referring to ASM and AD as a single interchangeable discipline is totally inappropriate. It is like thinking that civil engineering and electrical engineering are the same. Six differentiators highlighting the difference between the ASM discipline and the AD discipline are described below.

ASM vs AD #1: A Cultural Difference

Table 2 is an IT professional's perspective of the aspirational differences between a typical ASM programmer and a typical AD programmer. Superficially, AD programmers and ASM programmers are identical; both have the same skills and educational background. But as seen in Table 2, the similarities stop there.

TABLE 2. ASM vs AD: CULTURAL DIFFERENCE

	Applications Development (AD)	Applications Support and Maintenance (ASM)
Role in the Organization	Strategic, forward thinking	Operational, current thinking
Natural way of thinking	Projects and Technology	Assets (Applications) and Process
Source of pride within the organization	New technology to leverage the value of the business	Metrics showing continuous improvement
Inherent Capability	Visionary	Problem Solver
Methodology followed	Linear with defined beginning and end	Cyclical with no beginning or end
Personal Benchmarks	Project timelines and cost	Time to respond and time to resolve the incoming issues

ASM vs AD #2: Organization

FIGURE 2. ASM VS AD: IT ORGANIZATION CHART

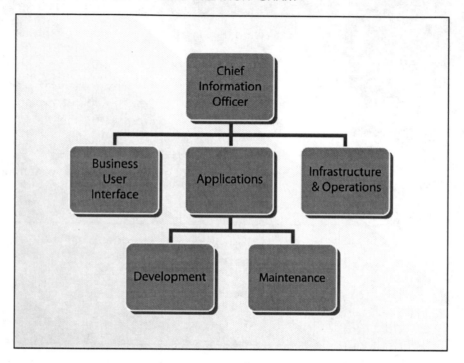

The sub-disciplines of the IT discipline are typically shown in an IT organization chart similar to Figure 2. But an IT organization chart is not helpful operationally. Operationally, one needs to see an IT Application Service Chain similar to the one shown in Figure 3. There, ASM is part of an Application Service Chain where Help Desk provides a service to Infrastructure who provides a service to ASM who provide a service to Power Users who provide a service to the end business users. AD is not part of this Service Chain. It is off to the side, responsible for replacing weak links in the service chain when required.

Figure 3. ASM Application Service Chain

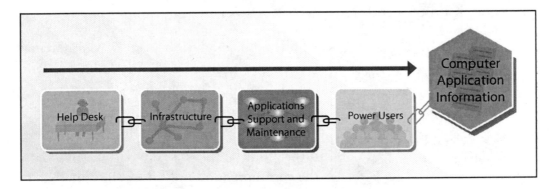

ASM vs AD #3: Governance

Infrastructure, Applications Development (AD), and Applications Support and Maintenance (ASM) each have different inherent governance models.

Infrastructure governance, because of the plethora of issues in multi-platform, multi-technology environments, operates as a theocracy. Standards reign supreme. Only certain technologies represented by certain vendors are permitted into the organization. Management promotes the selected technology with a religious fervor characteristic of theocracies and is merciless when putting down dissension and converting to the standard "religion." Non-believers must either convert or leave.

Applications Development (AD) governance is defined in the classic AD book, *The Mythical Man Month*, by Fredrick P. Brookes[4], as an aristocracy. Brookes says, "Conceptual integrity and architectural unity dictate that the design must proceed from one mind, or from a very small number of agreeing resonant minds." Data supports the claim that successful AD projects depend on implementing the vision of one or two people through an "arrogance of the aristocrats" approach to management. For success, the visionary, or leader, must have total control over all aspects of the project and dictatorial powers to

---

4   Frederick P Brookes, The Mythical Man Month, published 1995

ensure the right things are done at the right time. Hence, the AD governance model, to be successful, must resemble a dictatorship, or, as Brookes says in his book in a more gentle reference, an aristocracy.

Infrastructure = Theocracy

Application Development
= Aristocracy

Applications Support and
Maintenance = Democracy

Applications Support and Maintenance (ASM) governance inherently follows a democratic model. The charm of democracy for ASM is that the model excels in bringing disparate groups with competing requirements into a process, rule-based environment where the common good prevails. Being rule-based, overhead cost of direct management is minimal. ASM, as opposed to AD, is a flat organization. It is run by an application steering committee of "elected" representatives (application owners and stakeholders) who set priorities and provide overall direction to the custodians based on predefined rules set by the corporation.

ASM vs AD #4: Methodology, Tools, Certification

Every AD project has, by definition, a well-defined beginning and a well-defined end, linked together by a sequence of pre-planned tasks. Every AD methodology must therefore be based on the mathematical line.

ASM, by definition, has no beginning and no end. Every ASM methodology must therefore be based on a circle—the main mathematical symbol with no beginning and no end.

FIGURE 4. ASM LIFE CYCLE

FIGURE 5. AD LIFE CYCLE

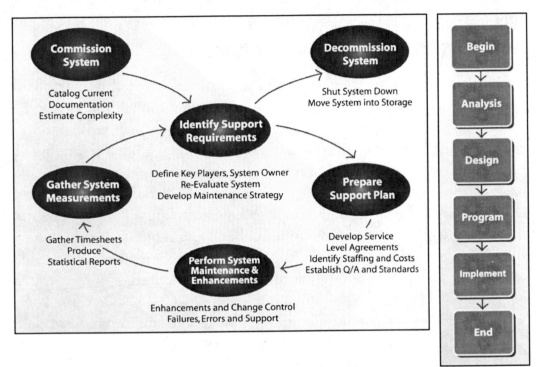

ASM work cannot be preplanned in the normal management sense. ASM work involves responding to and resolving what appear to be a series of unpredictable incidents, unanticipated problems, and unexpected enhancements. Predicting work in ASM is, however, possible. It is somewhat like predicting North American traffic accidents over a long weekend. Statisticians can accurately predict within a range how many accidents will occur. They just can't predict who will be involved, and exactly when and where each accident will occur.

In AD, of course, work is meticulously planned. We know months in advance exactly what each developer will be working on each day.

Hence, for tools, AD expects reports of actual progress against predefined schedules, deadlines, and costs as per any project management tool. ASM tools, on the other hand, are asset management tools (computer applications are assets) that accurately record asset activity (incidents, problems, enhance-ments) in a manner that supports continuous improvement. It is not unlike road accident data being used to continuously improve roads and cars.

ASM vs AD #5: Hiring and Inspiring Staff

Hittleman and Carr try to claim in their letter exchange that IT cost cut-ting and risk management (aka ASM) is not boring. But for the average IT professional, when compared to a career in the big-budget, high-paying, world-changing environment of Silicon Valley, ASM *is* boring. No self-respecting IT professional would ever admit to wanting a career in ASM…maintaining old programs written by "grandparents" using technology so old no professional has even heard of it. Attracting, keeping, and motivating IT professionals to the ASM discipline is and will continue to be an enormous challenge. It is the single most important consideration that could prove Carr's thesis wrong, and that might render CEO's powerless to change the current modus operandi in IT.

Below are seven recommendations on how to hire and inspire ASM staff. They are based on my thirty-year career in ASM, building a mid-sized con-sulting company focused exclusively on ASM.

Recommendation #1: Say what you do and do what you say.

Don't pretend you are an AD shop in order to attract IT staff if what you really do is ASM. A small minority of IT professionals really do like ASM and want to work with like-minded people. If you proclaim loudly and proudly that you are an ASM shop, you may attract these people.

Recommendation #2: Separate AD from ASM.

Keep the distinct disciplines, AD and ASM, separate but equal. Fight the IT per-ception that AD is high value and ASM is low value. For example, champagne and dinner with the president greet AD staff when a newly developed application goes into production, whereas the only time senior management meets the ASM staff is when some critical application has failed and they are angry and emotional.

Recommendation #3: Use fewer, better people and reward them.

Avoid the typical IT career perception of, "we will start you in ASM, and if you are good, we will promote you to AD." The door to the executive suite should not be restricted to those in AD. ASM should not be perceived as a place for juniors and under-achievers.

Recommendation #4: Improve the application environment.

Create an environment for attracting and keeping top-notch problem solvers. Instill the Problem Ownership Culture— see Best Practice #3.

Recommendation #5: Make the ASM job easier.

Avoid ASM organizational confusion where social skills become more important than technical skills when getting a problem solved or an application changed. Use the Black Box Delivery Model—see Best Practice #4.

Recommendation #6: Publish the metrics.

Million dollar athletes beg to participate for free in the Olympics because of one singular fact: Olympic metrics. CEO's trying to motivate ASM staff can learn from the Olympic metrics: immediately available, always accurate, unquestionably final, internationally recognized, and consistent over time; and they are not generated for shareholders, but for the athletes themselves.

Recommendation #7: Don't over-manage. Let the professionals follow the process.

ASM is a process that should just run. Once set up, minimal management attention is needed or desired. ASM inherently follows a democratic governance model and democracy demands a rule-based environment where there is extensive individual freedom. .

ASM vs AD #6: Functionality:

AD is the high risk, high investment, high leverage, leading-edge-technology undertaking represented by the top right corner of the diagram in Figure 6. ASM is the reliable, low cost, low risk, established technology represented by the bottom left corner of the same diagram.

From the perspective of Figure 6, the CIO's job is twofold:

1. Leverage the corporation through the new technology and AD of the top right corner.

2. As quickly as possible, shift all applications from the high-cost, unstable AD environment of the top right, to the low-cost, reliable ASM environment of the bottom left, and ultimately to decommissioning when they cease to add value.

FIGURE 6. ASM vs. AD FUNCTIONALITY

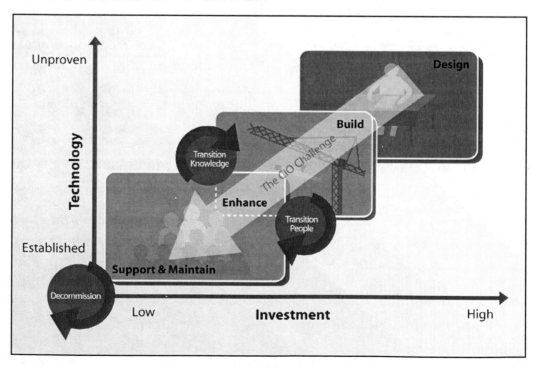

The CIO challenge in Figure 6 is that IT staff (and users) love the exciting big-budget, new-technology environment and strive to keep applications in the perpetual development mode of the top right corner. They insist (aided by the vendors, of course) that functional extensions, new projects, new versions, and technology upgrades are all value-added accomplishments, when in fact they may not be.

Even with ASM defined as different from AD, there is often still confusion within IT as to whether work being done on an application is AD or ASM. This confusion disappears when the computer application is viewed as a business asset. A business asset is either being acquired (AD mode) or being used (ASM mode). It cannot be in both modes at the same time. Similarly for computer applications—an application can only be in one mode: ASM or AD. It is the application owner who decides which mode the application is in.

The following aircraft carrier and hotel analogies exemplify this concept.

When an aircraft carrier is being built (or is undergoing major repairs) in the shipyard, it is like AD. There is a defined project with a beginning, an end, and a fixed one-time cost. There is no immediate value to this undertaking—it is an investment in the hope of obtaining value in the future. The owner (government) assigns a project manager who, using project management skills, methodologies, and tools, runs the project. His job is to manage through the sequence of pre-defined tasks and to complete the project on time and on budget.

When the same aircraft carrier, now built, is running in a theatre of war, it is like ASM. Preparing for and waging war is a process, without beginning and without end. It is run by a process expert (an admiral knowledgeable about how to wage war), whose job it is to defend the country and be ready and able to respond to random unpredictable events. The cost of operating the aircraft carrier is not one-time. It is an annual recurring cost that lasts so long as the aircraft carrier is in operation. The owner (government) continues to receive value (defense) from its original investment so long as the carrier stays out of the shipyard (AD).

Because there is only one ship, it is very clear when it is in the shipyard undergoing renovation (AD mode) versus when it is at sea under the command of its admiral (ASM mode). It can be in only one mode at a time and, ultimately, it is the owner (government) who decides which mode it is in. Similarly, a computer application can only be in one mode at a time, and it is the application owner who decides that mode.

A hotel analogy is no different. The person who designed and built the hotel is not the same person who manages the hotel and greets you when you arrive for check-in (unless it is a bed and breakfast, which are like small IT shops, so the analogy still holds). The hotel owners are also different from the custodians who run the day-to-day operation of the hotel. As in hotels, so too in applications: there are owners, there are customers (users), there were architects and builders long since gone and working on new hotel projects, and there are custodians (ASM) who look after the hotel day to day and keep it running.

A lack of distinction between ASM and AD is a fundamental obstacle for CIO's struggling to align to the business. Not viewing existing computer applications as valuable corporate assets for which they have custodianship, not ownership, will result in alignment challenges. Furthermore, a CIO who runs a shop of pure developers, who really are doing pure development, may not be providing any value to the corporation. Everything is always in development and there are no smooth-running applications that the organization can rely on. It is not unlike the aircraft carrier that is always in dry dock (AD mode) undergoing repairs. It is of absolutely no value to the owners (government) while in dry dock, and is in fact a drain on scarce resources that might be better deployed elsewhere. Also, any asset that is under constant development risks being obsolete before it is useful. CIO's who strive to proudly proclaim that a large percentage of their budget is AD are likely sadly misaligned with the wishes of their shareholders.

Finally, from a financial reporting perspective, CFO's must also understand and justify how the corporation accounts for ASM (reported as expense) versus AD (reported as capital). CFO's need total confidence that IT programmers, both ASM and AD, are charging their time appropriately. For accuracy and simplicity, clarity in rules for ASM versus AD are critical.

Implementation Challenges of ASM – the New IT Discipline

The source of the IT winds of change can be partially attributed to recent executive disillusionment with big applications development projects[5] and the business risk associated with revolutionary steps forward (as characterized by AD), versus the proven success in the use of incremental improvements as a management technique[6] (characterized by ASM). By applying the management principles of incremental improvement to IT through operational excellence in ASM, it can be argued that:

- Objectives can be reached without the risk and cost of new development;

- Existing systems can be made to last longer, thereby maximizing the value of the corporate asset and increasing the return on investment;

- Continued support and maintenance can be an alternative to software re-development—at least for the short term – thereby deferring costs.

- IT can be better aligned based on corporate processes than it can based on corporate projects.

The risk/benefit of these two opposing concepts is further illustrated in Tables 3 and 4 below.

5   Letter to the editor from John Seely Brown and John Hagel III, reprinted by permission of Harvard Business Review Press
6   The Deming Management Method; Mary Walton; Perigree Books, 1987
Building Continual Improvement, a Guide for Business; Donald J Wheeler and Sheila R Rowling;SPC Press, 1998

TABLE 3. TOP FIVE TECHNICAL ISSUES FACING THE CIO

1995	1996	1997
1. Client Server	1. Distributed Systems	1. Internet
2. Network	2. Network	2. ERP
3. Electronic Commerce	3. Data Warehousing	3. Data Warehousing
4. Application Development Tools	4. Work Group	4. Distributive Systems
5. Object Orientated Technologies	5. Client Server	5. Network

TABLE 4. TOP FIVE NON-TECHNICAL ISSUES FACING THE CIO

1995	1996	1997
1. Align IT to the Business Strategy	1. Align IT to the Business Strategy	1. Align IT to the Business Strategy
2. Using IT for competitive breakthroughs	2. Using IT for competitive breakthroughs	2. Using IT for competitive breakthroughs
3. Business and IT planning and architecture	3. Business and IT planning and architecture	3. Business and IT planning and architecture
4. Organization Strategies and Strategic Planning	4. Organization Strategies and Strategic Planning	4. Organization Strategies and Strategic Planning
5. Performance Metrics	5. Performance Metrics	5. Performance Metrics

During the late 90's, as tables 3 and 4 show, technology and technical issues were constantly changing thereby making executive decisions and prediction of future value of AD extremely difficult. Meanwhile, during the same period, the business issues remained unchanged and unresolved. These tables help explain the executive suite's current disillusionment with IT's previous focus on AD.

Hence, the impetus to move IT away from its traditional "project and technology" approach used in the great IT build-out over the past fifty years, to the more business operations approach of "asset and process". We can already sense these winds of change in IT today. For example, it is common practice to use packaged applications, and adjust business practices to fit these packages, rather than custom-building software to exactly fit current business practices. IT operational excellence via best practices in ASM seems to be a natural evolution going forward.

The crux in implementing ASM, the new IT discipline, is not just IT-related. As with any paradigm shift, it is not the shift itself, but the way management guides its corporation through the shift that creates lasting shareholder value. The following table summarizes the non-IT implications of implementing ASM as a new IT discipline.

TABLE 5. ASM: THE NEW IT PARADIGM

Observation (Paradigm Shift)	CEO Implication (action items)
IT consists of three distinct disciplines: ASM, AD, and Infrastructure.	Decide how you want to leverage, manage, and govern each of these distinct IT disciplines.
IT, when viewed as primarily ASM, is a cyclical process way of thinking, whereas IT, when viewed primarily as AD, is a sequence of projects way of thinking.	Decide how you want to align IT to your business. Either align IT to the business process or align IT to the corporate projects, and hire and inspire the IT staff accordingly.
ASM is a sub-service within an IT application service chain that in turn is a sub-service to a corporate service to end consumers.	Categorize IT assets into Application Service Chains linked to either a corporate service chain (for services) or corporate value chain (for products).
If the primary role of IT is ASM, then IT must adopt to the Operational Excellence operating model.	Identify both the corporate and IT operating models (Operational Excellence, Product Leadership, or Customer Intimate) and align accordingly.

If implementing ASM as a new IT discipline requires a shift in the whole IT operating model, the implications are immense. The challenges can be seen by taking a quick look at the 3 operating models summarized in the boxes below.

The Product Leadership Operating Model*	The Customer Intimate Operating Model*	The Operational Excellence Operating Model*
• A focus on the core processes of invention, product development and market exploitation.	• An obsession with the core processes of solutions development, results management, and relationship management.	• Processes for end-to-end... services that are optimized and streamlined to minimize costs and hassle
• A business structure that is loosely knit, ad hoc, and ever-changing to adjust to the entrepreneurial initiatives and redirections that characterize working in unexplored territory.	• A business structure that delegates decision-making to employees who are close to the customer.	• Operations that are standardized, simplified, tightly controlled, and centrally planned, leaving few decisions to the discretion of the rank-and-file employees.
• Management systems that are results-driven, that measure and reward new product successes, and that don't punish the experimentation needed to get there.	• Management systems that are geared toward creating results for carefully selected and nurtured clients.	• Management systems that focus on integrated, reliable, high-speed transactions and compliance to norms.
• A culture that encourages individual imagination, accomplishment, out-of-the-box thinking, and a mind-set driven by the desire to create the future	• A culture that embraces specific rather than general solutions and thrives on deep and lasting client relationships.	• A culture that abhors waste and rewards efficiency
IT Example: Plan, Build, Operate model with emphasis on Project Management and Project Delivery.	*IT Example: IT is totally decentralized with a separate CIO for each line of business, profit centre, significant business function and/or geographic area.*	*IT Example: Producer-Consumer** model where each producer, consumer is an IT discipline in an IT service chain centrally controlled by the CIO.*

* from The Discipline of Market Leaders, by Michael Treacy and Fred Wiersema.
** Producer-Consumer model is a well known software communication architecture used to describe interface standards between multiple independent software modules. Widely used in co-operative situations and multi-threaded programming.

As an example, a CEO who wants to move the IT way of thinking from the Product Leadership Operating Model (build mode) to the Operational Excellence Operating Model (operate mode), needs to take into consideration the following 7 items.

First: IT is not a single entity, just as engineering is not a single entity. A ninety-degree shift of IT from "build" to "operate" is like moving your engineering department from civil engineering to chemical engineering. Methodology, tools, people, culture, and management systems—all must change. Furthermore, moving from AD (the glorious, high-spending, revolutionize-the-world approach) to ASM (the mundane, reliable, useful, low-cost approach) will be a hard pill for IT to swallow. The change may destroy the existing IT organization.

Second: Moving your IT organization from Product Leadership (AD) to Operational Excellence (ASM) requires newly-built suites of enterprise-wide ASM standards, tightly controlled, centrally planned, and leaving few decisions to the rank and file employee. All IT and the whole enterprise must align to this centrally controlled standard. Unfortunately, few if any corporations have these industrial strength ASM standards in-house. They must be created.

Third: If the enterprise is not experienced in rolling out standardized procedures to the entire corporation, IT is not a good place to start. See Appendix I for examples of standardized procedures. Implementing new standards is a challenge, even in the most accepting of corporate cultures. Trying to roll out a new suite of centrally controlled ASM procedures to IT, known for its ingrained product leadership culture, without the support and experience of operational excellence in the corporate culture, would be an extremely challenging task.

Fourth: Considering the immense differences, it will be difficult to successfully manage the two IT disciplines, ASM and AD, within the same organization. Selectively outsourcing an IT discipline may have to be considered, and, given its commodity characteristics, ASM is a better suited candidate. Given its strategic importance, companies should be highly selective when outsourcing AD, doing so only when the level of business knowledge required is higher outside the organization.

Fifth: The "IT shop till you drop culture" of AD is not necessarily restricted to the IT department. IT shopaholics with budgets and authority can reside throughout an entire organization; if the corporate culture permits, these user shopaholics will spend more on IT than IT itself. Hence, it is not just IT that must change from a "technology leadership paradigm" to an "alert followership paradigm." The whole company must change. The following hype index diagram in figure 7 has been used by some corporations to help them through this cultural shift.

FIGURE 7. HYPE INDEX

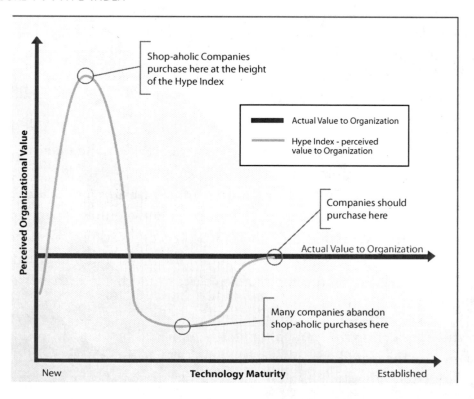

Sixth: For this immense undertaking to be successful, the whole management team must be on board. The CEO must persuade the whole company that its competitive advantage in IT lies in having an evolutionary, continuous improvement, approach (characterized by ASM) versus a revolutionary step forward approach (characterized by AD). If the whole organization does not embrace this concept, the change from "build mode" to "operate mode" will be extremely difficult to implement successfully.

Seventh: Most importantly, the CEO and executive team must remember that "ASM: the new IT discipline" really is new! And because it is new and immature, it carries the normal risk-reward attributes of any new concept.

Figure 8, detailed in Appendix H, shows how the three primary IT disciplines: ASM, AD and infrastructure interact through a typical corporate planning cycle.

FIGURE 8. IT MANAGEMENT MODEL FOR OPERATIONAL EXCELLENCE

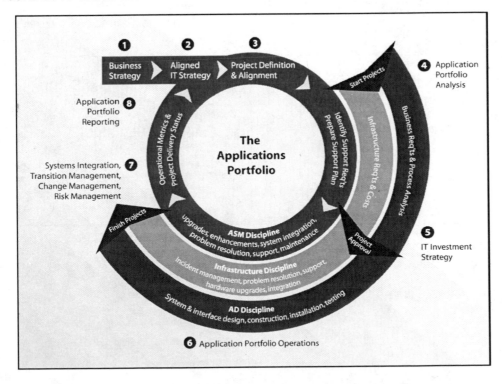

This concludes a management overview of Applications Support and Maintenance – the New IT Discipline. Simplistically, the discipline is a riveted focus on the installed base of applications – making them reliable, useful and low-cost.

The next four chapters in this book focus on the ASM discipline. They are an introductory **How To** for implementing operational excellence in IT using twelve best practices in ASM. The twelve best practices are organized in chapters based on the framework shown in Figure 9 below.

FIGURE 9. THE ASM TWELVE BEST PRACTICES

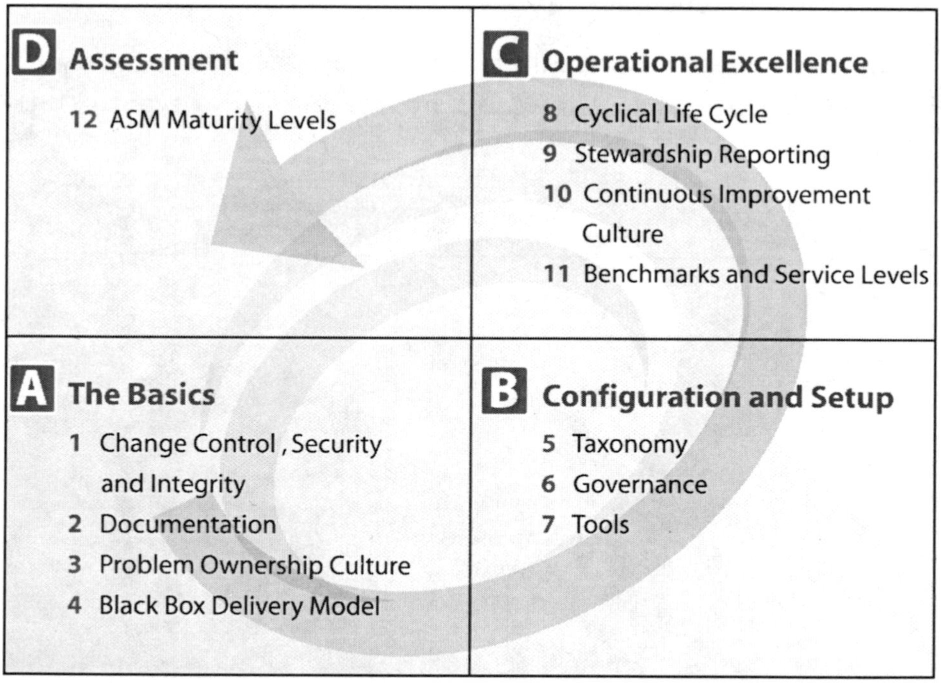

D **Assessment**

    12 ASM Maturity Levels

C **Operational Excellence**

    8 Cyclical Life Cycle
    9 Stewardship Reporting
    10 Continuous Improvement Culture
    11 Benchmarks and Service Levels

A **The Basics**

    1 Change Control , Security and Integrity
    2 Documentation
    3 Problem Ownership Culture
    4 Black Box Delivery Model

B **Configuration and Setup**

    5 Taxonomy
    6 Governance
    7 Tools

Chapter 2

THE BASICS: WHAT EVERYONE SHOULD KNOW AND PRACTICE

In ASM there are four fundamental best practices that represent the "must do" of ASM, irrespective of value discipline, operating model, or business strategy. They are the basics of the whole ASM discipline and must be followed—always:

1. ASM Best Practice #1: Change Control, Security, and Integrity

2. ASM Best Practice #2: Documentation

3. ASM Best Practice #3: Problem Ownership Culture

4. ASM Best Practice #4: Black Box Delivery Model

These four best practices are truly basic. To repeat: they must be followed everywhere and by everyone, irrespective of a company's size, location, or sophistication. They are equally applicable to mission critical applications running in billion dollar enterprises and to tiny applications running on a home PC. Again: they are very, very basic and must be implemented before advanced concepts around ASM Operational Excellence are introduced.

Best Practice #1
Change Control,
Security, and Integrity

Software, if not modified, runs exactly the same every time. It never wears out. Best Practice #1: Change Control, Security, and Integrity is based on this premise: "Protect what you know works, so you can go back to it if necessary." Best practice #1 is a set of nine rules that must be followed in every ASM environment.

Rule #1 – Back-out Rule:

Before making any change to a publicly used computer environment, one must be totally confident that, should the change not work, it can easily be backed out of the environment in a reasonable amount of time, and everything can be returned to exactly the way it was before the change was implemented. If there is any chance of being unable to return to the previous environment, the change must not be attempted without prior knowledge and acceptance of the risk by the public user community. Sometimes the back-out rule involves being able to re-install software from scratch in a reasonable amount of time. Usually the back-out rule capability is handled through a combination of rules #5 and #6.

Rule #2 – Data Integrity Rule:

All data must be backed up on a regular cycle (daily, weekly, or monthly) and locked safely away. Data transactions between backups must be kept so that one can re-create all data from a backup in a reasonable amount of time should the current version be corrupted. In small home-PC environments, data should be regularly copied onto CDs to prevent inadvertent loss.

Rule #3 – Testing Rule:

Nothing, absolutely *nothing*, is implemented into a publicly used computer environment without first testing it in a non-public environment and then gaining acceptance that the test works. There must be reasonable assurance that the change will work before it is implemented for public use. This rule explains why downloading and installing unapproved or untested software from the Internet is frowned upon in corporate environments. To use a medical analogy: do your experiments on lab rats, not the general population.

Rule #4 – Source Code Integrity Rule:

If you are building or using software developed in-house, then for all production code (in-house software actively being used by the organization) there must be corresponding source code (human readable versions of the production code) that exactly matches the production code. This rule is fundamental. It is paramount that its principles are adhered to. To guarantee integrity, production versions of source/production code must be locked safely away from all unauthorized access. There must be strict and secure processes for accessing copies of source/production code. Check-out/check-in processes must guarantee that only one programmer (or managed group of programmers) is changing source code (and corresponding production code) at a single point in time. (see rule #5). Note that for purchased software, it is the software vendor who must maintain the integrity of the source code.

Rule #5 – Separate Environment Rule:

In large IT organizations, where there are distinct usages of the same software, separate environments must exist for separate functions. Thus, production, test, acceptance, training, sales, and whatever other functions exist in the organization for the software—all need separate environments. Each environment must be totally independent from every other so that if changes are made in one environment, there is no impact on the function of another environment. Each subsidiary environment must replicate or emulate the production environment (always the master environment) in sufficient detail to perform its function effectively. In addition, established "promotion control" processes must exist to enable updates from one environment to another.

Rule #6 – Separation of Duties Rule:

In large IT organizations, production control analysts who are responsible for the security and integrity of "in production" code are not permitted to make any changes to any application code or data. Programmers who are responsible for all application changes are not permitted access to "in production" code and must work with copies provided by production control analysts. "Acceptance testing" and "permission to move to production" tasks are the sole responsibility of the user (owner) of the application. Users are not permitted to change applications or access "in production" code.

Rule #7 – Window of Opportunity Rule:

Changes to publicly used computer environments must never occur unannounced. The change must occur when the public users are fully aware that a change will occur—for example, on a regular cycle (every Wednesday night) or on a pre-selected day that has minimal impact on normal operation. The greater the risk associated with the change, the greater the public awareness needs to be. The change should occur such that there is the longest window of time possible (e.g. a weekend when the application is not used) to recover should the change not work. In other words, changes to publicly used computer environments must be planned and coordinated.

Rule #8 – Change Control Process Rule:

Strict change control processes must be followed when making a change to "in production" source code and corresponding production code. There can be more than one change control process to reflect different situations. Two typical change control processes are:

- *Normal Change Control Process:* Used for normal change. Note that "normal change" does not permit change to a production environment. It requires strict adherence to the "test, acceptance, promotion to production" control process.

- *Emergency Change Control Process:* Used in emergency situations where the application is not working and immediate change directly to the production environment is imperative. Although the change is done immediately using "emergency mode powers," at a later point in time, when things are under control, a post mortem is done where the "access, change, and implement change in production" process is audited to ensure it meets the requirements of rules #5 and #6.

An example of a normal change control process is shown in Table 6.

TABLE 6: EXAMPLE OF AN ASM NORMAL CHANGE CONTROL PROCESS

Action	Explanation	Party
1. A programmer checks out a copy of the application source code	While the source code is checked out, no one else can access the source code (except for view only). This avoids changes on top of changes issues.	Production Control
2. Make source code change and complete testing on local machine – the **Test Environment**	This testing is done locally on the programmer's machine (or in a separate test environment)	Programmer
3. Move change (source code plus production code) to **Acceptance Environment**	Programmer does not have access to the source code in Acceptance Environment.	Production Control
4. Test change in Acceptance Environment and signoff the change	Acceptance Environment is locked.	Originator
5. Move source code and production code to **Production Environment**	Before copying anything over top of the existing Production Environment, a complete copy of existing environment is backed up. If there is a problem with the change, the previous environment is restored.	Production Control

Rule # 9 – Backup Recovery Rule:
    Exact replicas of the production environment must exist offsite such that one is able to re-create the environment from scratch, starting with brand new hardware as if a fire had wiped everything out the night before. A formal disas-

ter recovery plan (DRP) with disaster recovery procedures describing how to recover an application from its backup must be documented. This is usually a part of a broader business continuity and recovery plan covering contingencies for the entire business. Regularly scheduled physical backups of all databases and programs must occur so that recovery time and effort is minimized.

Note that irrespective of how rigorously Best practice #1 and the other ASM best practices are followed, software reliability can never be 100 percent guaranteed. As with anything, design flaws and glitches introduced during original design or development can remain hidden, only to be triggered by an unpredictable series of events. What ASM best practices do provide is increased reliability over time as the application glitches are first found and then safely and efficiently removed with minimal business impact. That said, if possible, it is still better to start using an application after its ASM best practices have been long since established and after most glitches have been removed. Hence the oft-quoted management recommendation for IT—follow, don't lead.

Best Practice #2
Documentation

Documentation states that every ASM organization, from global billion-dollar company to individual home PC user, must retain sufficient documentation about their publicly used computer environment so that if a problem occurs or a change is needed, the problem/change can be handled intelligently. Furthermore, this documentation must be organized so that if necessary, it can be passed to third-party ASM programmers so that they also can handle problems and/or changes intelligently.

Modern ASM documentation is a set of tickets (records if you prefer) describing all ASM activity recorded against each and every application in the application inventory. ASM tickets are like a ship's log, or a patient's medical chart, or an automobile's maintenance record. They describe activity around and about the computer application asset, but they do not describe the computer application itself—just as a ship's log kept by the captain is not the ship's specifications, or the automobile's maintenance record is not the automobile's engineering design. The analogy follows with computer applications. ASM tickets describe the "medical" history of each application. As in medicine, without a history of problems, changes, and enhancements (illnesses, treatments, and operations) the ASM programmer (doctor) is reluctant to apply more changes and fixes. Working in the dark without a history of problems and changes is extremely risky—for both ASM professionals and medical professionals.

IT documentation has been traditionally AD-oriented, with computer application documentation defined as an external description of what source code does—often a derivative of the original design specifications. This approach to ASM documentation is—thankfully—a thing of the past. Writing cryptic programs in even more cryptic languages without internal comments has been driven from the IT discipline. By using internal comments with structured programming techniques, modern descriptive languages, and encapsulation, most programs can be written and read like a book and have no need of separate documentation to interpret the source code. Programs today are like university math textbooks—completely incomprehensible to the uninitiated but invaluable reference material for the professional. Neither needs burdening with additional material that is often dated, inaccurate, and unreliable.

Note that best practice #2 defines only ASM-specific documentation needed by ASM practitioners in the support, maintenance, and enhancement of applications. Other application related documentation is as follows:

- AD documentation showing original design specifications, and major enhancement specifications for the computer application.

- Application user documentation in the form of user manuals, online help, marketing collateral showing the overall architecture of the application and data; and work flow diagrams showing how users interact with various applications at various points of time in a business cycle.

- Infrastructure documentation showing servers, terminals, software, and users and the network interconnection for the infrastructure on which the application runs.

- Executive information needed for governance and management of the application environment, described later in this book.

A guideline showing ASM documentation needed in key environments in order to resolve issues, handle problems, and institute change is described in table 7.

TABLE 7. DOCUMENTATION BEST PRACTICE GUIDELINES

Environment	Documentation Needed in this Environment to Handle a Problem/Change Intelligently
For every PC owner	Keep all computer records in a desk drawer: licenses, warrantees, purchase invoices, user guides and other documents received when hardware and software is purchased.
	Create a spreadsheet of hardware, and the software and applications you installed highlighting the information needed for getting help on each product – phone number, web site, model or license information they need to answer your call.
	Keep all the passwords, computer names, software naming conventions, and setup information and conventions you used for all installation and setup of the computer stored safely. Be comfortable that if unresolvable problems with your computer occur, you know how to re-create your computer environment from scratch by erasing the hard disk and re-installing all software from scratch.
A small ASM shop (1 to 3 programmers) with external infrastructure support	Ticket documentation is a manually kept log of application issues identifying: • Application name • Date and time of occurrence of incident • Summary of the issue in as few words as possible • A separate more detailed description of the issue and the action taken • Name of the person writing in the log entry and name of person who is handling the situation.

A large IT organization	Tickets are organized according to a universal application taxonomy or classification system, showing the relative urgency or priority, using ASM-specific computer application reporting tools.
	Other documents to report ASM activity to management (Stewardship Report), explain the business environment to IT programmers (Immersion Manual), and provide on-call specific information for programmers (Application Support Binder) are also important.
A large sophisticated IT organization	Tickets showing response time, resolve time, estimated time, and actual time, all compared to an industry benchmark.

Best Practice #3
Problem Ownership
Culture

Problem Ownership Culture states that computer applications must be reliable. Applications with bugs, errors, crashes, and inconsistencies should either be fixed or retired from use.

Because it is a cultural best practice for ASM professionals, best practice #3 means there is an underlying theme within the profession where disruptive bugs, errors, crashes, and inconsistencies, irrespective of where they occur, are an embarrassment to the ASM profession; ASM programmers who perpetuate these environments are ostracized. Furthermore, all ASM practitioners and programmers inherently avoid situations where there is risk of introducing disruptive problems. If a problem does occur, they take personal responsibility for getting rid of the problem so that it never re-occurs.

Every discipline has an underlying themed culture that permeates all aspects of the profession. This culture dictates how society expects practitioners of the discipline to act and respond—behavior so inherent and ingrained that it becomes a code of conduct expected by everyone. For medicine it is the culture of saving lives, irrespective of who it is; for engineers it is the culture of safety in design; for accountants it is the culture of accuracy in numbers; and for ASM it is the culture of problem-free, smooth-running, reliable applications—the problem ownership culture. If there is a problem in an application, then the whole ASM profession owns it and is responsible for fixing it.

At a day to day practical level, problem ownership culture within an organization's ASM means:

- When a customer calls for support, the ASM service team must assume full responsibility and ownership for resolving that problem to the satisfaction of the caller (business user, help desk, or whoever requested the fix);

- When application problems occur, even without customer calls, the ASM team becomes advocates for resolving these problems and their root causes by presenting a case for its resolution to the application owner;

- When the resolution of a problem lies fully within its responsibilities, an ASM service team must utilize its resources to identify the root cause of the problem and resolve it in a manner so that the problem never re-occurs;

- When the resolution to a problem lies outside of their responsibilities, ASM team members must become the problem's advocate, taking steps to assign the problem to the correct support group and ensuring that group assumes ownership to resolve the problem at their level.

- If there is no existing procedure, the problem-solving culture should push for the institution of a common problem-solving process for others to use.

The problem ownership culture evolves computer applications into something the ASM profession is culturally proud of: applications that run smoothly day after day without need of intervention by programmers.

Best Practice #4
Black Box
Delivery Model

Black Box Delivery Model states formally that all computer applications, for purposes of ASM custodianship responsibility, must be encapsulated so that responsibility for smooth operation is the responsibility of one and only one team of ASM programmers.

Informally, "black box" is an engineering term used to describe a system or process that is extremely complex and difficult to understand on the inside, but very simple on the outside. The use of the term black box in engineering serves two fundamental purposes:

- It allows engineers to design and maintain the complex process from the inside, while everyday users can simply use the process on the outside; and

- Black box enables humans to create immensely complex machines (e.g. the space shuttle) otherwise considered beyond the realm of possibility. All complex machines in engineering are made up of many individual, complex sub-machines, and can be assembled simply by linking individual black boxes together. By definition, the details of an immensely complex machine cannot be understood (and therefore not designed or built) by a single individual.

The use of the term black box in IT allows applications to be separated into distinct black boxes, linked together, which enables one and only one application support team to be responsible for all changes to that application black box. The application support team then becomes an expert on their black box application. If several teams were permitted to make changes to applications within the black box, the integrity of the application black box source code would be extremely difficult to maintain, rendering ASM difficult, expensive, and demoralizing.

For the application owner, the outputs from the black box are smoothly running applications with high reliability, uptime, and performance. His/her inputs to the black box are two budgetary items as shown in figure 10:

- *Long Term Fixed Price Support and Maintenance (often called Expense Budget):* The ASM budget, which is agreed to each year by the application owner as part of the cyclical application lifecycle. This number represents a headcount for the year that the application support team must dedicate to supporting this application black box. Headcount is the key metric used by application owners to manage ASM custodial costs because it is the major cost input to any ASM service provider.

- *Pre-approved Enhancements (often called Capital Budget):* Represents additional funds above plan that may be required for additional headcount if additional enhancements or sub-contract development are needed and cost/benefit-justified. Normal processes for obtaining additional funding must be followed. In other words, this number represents additional headcount that must be temporarily added to the ASM service provider team to meet demands for extra, unplanned work.

If ASM managers must manage based on cost/value as well as headcount, capital versus expense can be somewhat complex with depreciation and capital cost allowance. Sometimes, accountants will "hide" the intricacies of depreciation expense and capital cost allowance and allow the ASM discipline to use simple cash-accounting principles for managing capital.

Typical ASM Management Metrics	
ASM Cost:	Headcount
ASM Value:	Time to Respond
	Time to Resolve

An important benefit of the black box delivery model is that it enables good old "pride in ownership." Everyone likes to be able to look at something and claim ownership.

Figure 10. Black Box Delivery Model

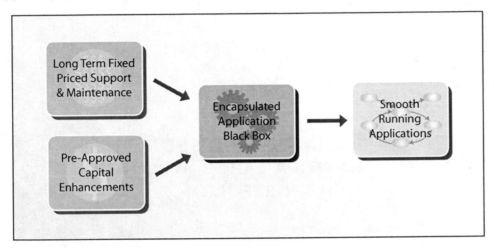

This concludes the basics of ASM best practices. With rigor and discipline around just these four basic ASM best practices, individuals with home PCs and small IT shops with fewer than ten employees can expect reliable, useful, low-cost computer applications. Equally applicable to large enterprises with big application portfolios, these four basic ASM best practices should be truly universal.

The next two chapters, *Configuration and Setup* and *Operational Excellence*, describe an ASM best practice framework for large complex IT environments. The best practices in these chapters represent a suite of ASM standards that are industrial-strength, enterprise-wide, and that can be centrally managed and controlled. They are the hallmark of operational excellence in IT.

Chapter 3

CONFIGURATION AND SETUP: HOW TO ORGANIZE A LARGE APPLICATION PORTFOLIO

Configuration and Setup, ASM best practices #5 to #7, enables the company to get a handle on the computer application assets it owns and operates. It provides standard terminology thereby setting the stage for a common understanding of business value of every application in the corporation. This enables all staff, not just IT staff, to eliminate waste (remove duplicate, low value, un-used applications), reduce risk (ensure mission critical applications are identified in the business continuity plan), and maximize use and value of the installed base of computer applications. When centralized ASM process and procedures (described in the next chapter *Operational Excellence*, ASM best practices #8 – #11) are added, IT operational excellence is achieved. It is a large undertaking but well worth the effort. Too often, the corporation's application portfolio and the supporting procedures are a technological quagmire that few business leaders and staff even want to try to understand.

Details within the ASM configuration and setup best practices are a means to drive the corporation through a process which aligns the application portfolio and ASM delivery environment with corporate lines of business and overall strategy, without diluting any of the ASM best practices. The modis operandi of these ASM best practices is to first analyze, align and configure, and then set up and store the complexity of the corporation's applications and

ASM services in data repositories. Once configured and stored, these data repositories become the unchanging standard around which ASM Operational Excellence is built. The ASM Twelve Best Practices, aligned with corporate strategy and culture, digitally encoded in the ASM tool, are standard worthy of rollout to the enterprise.

Configuration and setup of an ASM environment requires enterprise-wide decisions on the following ASM standards:

1. The corporate application portfolio structure, viewed and reported in a manner that makes sense to everyone in the enterprise.

2. The standard enterprise-wide ASM task list for support, maintenance, and enhancement of the application portfolio that again makes sense to everyone in the enterpise.

3. The standard ASM procedures to be followed by all ASM practitioners charged with performing ASM tasks.

4. The standard ASM team structure defining the corporate intellectual capital needed to keep an enterprise application running in perpetuity without need of management intervention. The team structure is cross functional and non-organizational in that anyone from anywhere, inside or outside the company, can be part of the team.

5. The standard enterprise-wide governance process to set priorities and resolve conflicts.

The first three items—application portfolio, ASM task list, and ASM procedures—are defined in the taxonomy best practice. The subsequent two items, ASM team structure and ASM governance, are defined in the governance best practice.

Best Practice #5
Taxonomy

For ASM to exist as a viable discipline, we need to be able to communicate in a common, well-understood, and widely used language—ASMeese, if you will—ASM-specific words, descriptions, and terminology where we all agree on the definition.

The importance of taxonomy in any discipline is exemplified by the Dilbert-like dialogue between two people shown below.

> "A whale is a fish."
> "No its not, it's a mammal."
> "A whale is a fish! It swims like a fish, it looks like a fish. It is definitely a fish"
> "No it's not. It's a mammal. Everyone knows it's a mammal".
> "People are mammals, dogs are mammals. A whale can't walk on land. It has no legs. It's definitely not a mammal. It must be a fish."
> "But fish lay eggs and have gills to breathe underwater. To be fish, whales would have to have gills and lay eggs. It can't be a fish"
> "Well it can't be a mammal. Just because it doesn't lay eggs or have gills doesn't make it a mammal. I still think it's a fish."
> "Whales have babies. Humans have babies. Whales breathe air. Humans breathe air. They are very much like humans and dogs. They are mammals.
> "Say what you like. You will never convince me a whale is a mammal. It just looks too much like a fish. It will just confuse people if we call it a mammal when it looks like a fish."
> "But it really is a mammal. Don't look on the outside of the whale. Look on the inside."
> "Well I'm the boss and we need a decision so from now on, a whale is a fish."
> "But I just checked with the VP who is your boss and she says a whale is a mammal"
> "My boss and I haven't reached a conclusion on this discussion yet. Until we do, a whale is a fish. This discussion needs to be opened up to others. Perhaps a whale-is-a-fish committee needs to be formed."
>
> … and so the wasted time and circular discussion continues on and on, escalating within the organization, and wasting even more time in silly, unproductive discussions.

The word "taxonomy" comes from biology, and means classification. Biologists use taxonomy to describe life on Earth—one of the most complex of realities to define. There will always be the duck-billed platypus arguments—is it a mammal or a bird? But biologists are firm on their taxonomy and don't let the occasional duck-billed platypus deter them from enforcing the taxonomy. The alternative is total anarchy—which is often the case in ASM environments. As in biology, so in ASM; with a solid taxonomy, pointless discussions around definitions shouldn't occur.

The ASM taxonomy defined in best practice #5 provides everyone with a common understanding of the corporation's application portfolio and the work needed to support this portfolio. It eliminates the confusion around requests, procedures, and types of applications. It provides IT and application owners/users and executives across the enterprise a consistent means of communicating ASM requirements and objectives.

The ASM Taxonomy is made up of two components:

- The *ASM Master Taxonomy* is the universal backbone on which all ASM configurations and setup are based. During setup and configuration, the ASM Master Taxonomy acts as a checklist to ensure nothing is inadvertently missed or forgotten in the ASM environment.

- The *ASM Local Configuration* is the local business implementation of the ASM Twelve Best Practices mapped to the ASM Master Taxonomy. It is set up to use local business terminology and to align to the local way of thinking. In other words, ASM Local Configuration enables ASM to align with the business without diluting the ASM discipline's best practices as defined in its methodology, tools and certification.

The fast food analogy shown in Table 8 helps explain the relationship between Master Taxonomy and Local Configuration.

TABLE 8. FAST FOOD TAXONOMY

Local Configuration	Master Taxonomy
Big Mac™	Hamburger
HarveyBurger™	Hamburger
Whopper™	Hamburger
Wendy's Old Fashioned Burger™	Hamburger
Coke™	Soft Drink
Pepsi™	Soft Drink
Sprite™	Soft Drink

The configuration and setup process for the Master Taxonomy and the Local Configuration are shown in Figure 11. It is subsequently described in detail.

FIGURE 11. CONFIGURATION AND SETUP TAXONOMY

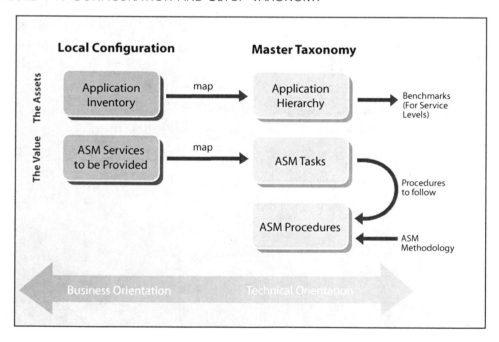

ASM Master Taxonomy

The ASM Master Taxonomy is comprised of three separate sub-taxonomies that define the key aspects of ASM configuration and setup:

Master Application Hierarchy:

Defines a three-level hierarchy representing three levels of abstraction, each describing the exact same total content[7] of the application inventory but to three different levels of management in the company:

- *Level Blue Applications*: This is the highest level of abstraction in the application hierarchy. It is the complete application inventory described in terms of business functions that align totally with the business. Level Blue applications are used by business executives for all application strategy planning, costing, governance, service levels, and stewardship reporting. Level Blue applications represent the lines of business, value chain activities, profit centers, or significant business functions all common within an industry, as in "banking mortgages applications."

- *Level Green Applications*: This is the middle level of abstraction in the application hierarchy used to bridge the gap between technical staff and business executives. Application owners and business users within each business function use this level of abstraction to communicate work requests to the technical staff (issues, problems, enhancements—i.e. tickets) and the priorities of these work requests. They also use this level of abstraction to interpret the strategic priorities and investment strategies to the technical staff.

- *Level Yellow Applications:* This is the lowest level of abstraction in the application hierarchy. It is the complete application inventory described in technology terms such as programs, modules, packages, and subroutines. All computer technical staff, such as programmers, production control

---

7   Total content reporting capability means the ability to generate an automated report that reflects the entire contents of the data repository thereby providing a complete picture. Important for auditing and e-MBWA – management by walking around not the shop floor but the data repositories.

analysts, and vendor support analysts, use this level of abstraction for communication. It is at this level of abstraction that all physical changes are made to implement the operational changes requested via tickets.

The Master Application Taxonomy also pre-defines two standard application attributes: application importance and skill-set. Skill-set, the training and expertise needed to understand the application's underlying technology, is also organized in a hierarchy (see Appendix A).

Application Hierarchy for an
Oil and Gas Exploration and Production Company**

Level Blue Applications
(Profit center, line of business, or significant business function)
1. **Exploration**
2. **Production Accounting**
3. **General Accounting**
4. **HR and Payroll**

Level Green Applications (commonly known application name)

Exploration	Production Accounting	General Accounting	HR and Payroll
AccuMap	Prism	ACCTDB	PeopleSoft
XPLOR	Atlas2000	FLOW	
DDF		PEEP	

Level Yellow Applications (Program Modules)

Accumap	Accudocs99, Accuin04, Accuput, Accutak
XPLOR	Xdb, Xrender, XLBS
DDF	DDFv6.3
Prism	Wellview, Wellgen, AssetBook, Whip, BudgetTool
Atlas2000	AtlasV4.4
ACCTDB	ACCT V3.7
FLOW	Wellflow, testflow,
PEEP	PEEPCan, PEEPUSA, PEEPSaudi
PeopleSoft	ePerformance, ePay, eProfile, eBenefits, Global Payroll
** NOTE: This is not real data	

Master Tasks Taxonomy:

Classifies tasks attributes into five categories. Most of these categories are needed to identify which procedure to follow in the ASM methodology. They are:

- *Task Type:* Problem, enhancement, data fix, and information request.

- *Task Lifecycle:* Received, responded, resolved.

- *Task Priority:* Critical, high, normal.

- *Task Value:* Good work, bad work. For example, scheduled enhancements (good) versus unexpected problems (bad).

- *Task Occurrence:* Business hours, after hours.

These are described in more detail in Appendix A.

Master Procedures Taxonomy:

Identifies a set of ASM procedures to follow based on best practices. An ASM environment must have an ASM methodology documenting in detail the following four procedures. These procedures must be online—and automatically linked to by the ASM toolset so that when a ticket is entered or viewed, the correct procedure to follow is presented immediately.

- *Support Procedure:* This is the procedure that everyone thinks of when talking about help desk or ITIL (Information Technology Infrastructure Library). It is often referred to as incident management. It classifies each call that is received (incident in ITIL), and tries to route it to the proper process and person based on its classification.

Support is normally divided into levels where:

1. Level 1 Support is normally handled by a help desk.

2. Level 2 support is an escalation of the call to a person in the appropriate discipline—ASM, Infrastructure, or Power Users—because it is too complex for the level one support person to handle. This is where the ASM discipline picks up responsibility for ASM support requests and puts them through the ASM-specific support procedure.

3. Level 3 Support is an escalation within the discipline to recognized experts – the last line of defense, so to speak, in solving the problem.

- *Enhancement Procedure:* Enhancements are small[8] development projects that improve the functionality and usability of the application. The key ASM enhancement procedure is the prioritization process as described in Best Practice #6: Governance. Otherwise, this procedure is similar to a development project procedure.

- *Change Procedure:* This is the procedure followed when application software is changed. All changes with respect to ASM are classified into two types:

  1. Emergency Change: Followed when the system is broken and not working.

  2. Normal Change: Followed in most circumstances.

  Best practices states that one of these two change procedures *must* be followed when making *any* change to the application! This includes enhancements, new development modules, and support fixes. There must be absolutely no exceptions, irrespective of who or why the change is being made.

- *Transition Procedure:* There are two ASM transition procedures:

  1. Transition from development to ASM.

  2. Transition from one ASM service provider to another.

  The complete ASM Master Taxonomy is shown in Appendix A.

ASM Local Configuration

ASM Local Configuration is a business alignment process. Simply, it layers the corporate value chain, which is strategic, over top of the application

---

8 Small development project is an often used but misleading term. Enhancements can be very large development projects being managed by the ASM team. It is not the project size that differentiates ASM from AD, but rather the application mode set by the application owner as described in Chapter One's ship analogy "in dry dock or at sea." Size has nothing to do with differentiating ASM work from AD work.

service chain, which is operational. This overlay process aligns the application service chain and all of its components to the corporate value chain and all its components. Once aligned, business management is able to leverage value from its computer application assets using the identical management techniques used to manage any other asset.

ASM Local Configuration and setup requires configuration of three elements: applications, services, and people. ASM processes and procedures are part of the ASM discipline and should not be changed from the Master Procedures Taxonomy.

- *Configure Applications:* Organize the plethora of computer applications into the three-level application hierarchy. The Level Blue applications must align with the lines of business in the corporate value chain. The Level Green and Level Yellow applications are placed in the hierarchy accordingly. Attributes of the application needed by the business are added at each level. The application importance attribute is added to enable benchmarking as per best practice #11. The application technology attribute is selected from the skills hierarchy shown in Appendix A.

- *Configure Services:* List the application services that will create value to the line of business. Map these services to the Master Task Taxonomy for purposes of ASM procedures, benchmarks, and best practices.

- *Configure People:* Create application custodianship teams using the application technology (skill-set) hierarchy, knowledge repository, and master team structure. Both technical and business knowledge must be taken into consideration. Create the application governance committees in a similar manner.

The result of ASM local configuration setup is shown in figure 12, and is described in detail below.

FIGURE 12. ASM CONFIGURATION AND SETUP

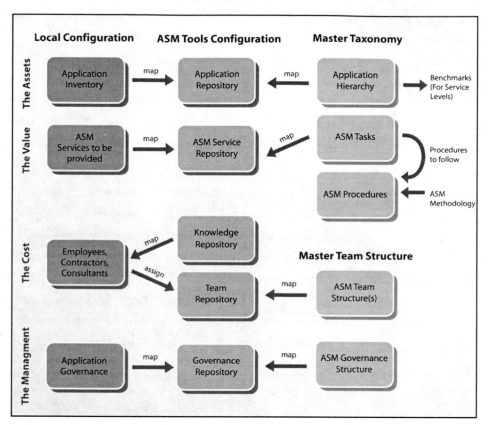

Locally Configured Application Inventory (see figure 12): A listing of all applications in the corporation in a three-level hierarchy using naming conventions as follows:

a)   Level Blue: Line of business or value chain terminology understood both internally and externally.

b)   Level Green: Internal commonly-used names of applications.

c)   Level Yellow: Technical names used by programmers.

Any one of the three levels can be used to completely describe all applications in the whole portfolio.

Locally Configured ASM Services To Be Provided (see figure 12): Describing which ASM services will be provided (and by omission which services will not be provided), thereby aligning to the business investment strategy. For example, during times of financial cutbacks, enhancements may be an ASM service that is no longer provided..

Locally Configured Employees, Contractors, Consultants (see figure 12): Identifying individuals assigned specific roles for specific applications within the predefined corporate ASM Team structure. The skill-set of the team, mapped against application technology highlights skills gaps.

Locally Configured Application Governance (see figure 12): Identifying corporate individuals responsible for the application as per the corporate ASM Governance structure.

TABLE 9. ASM TAXONOMY SUMMARY

ASM Taxonomy Summary
ASM requirements for the corporation are defined and shown as lists of: • Assets (Application hierarchy in terms of the master taxonomy) • Activity (Locally Configured Services, or Master Taxonomy Tasks – submitted using Tickets) • Procedures (documented process to follow when an activity is performed on an asset)

Best Practice #6
Governance

Governance is government and government is governance. The ASM governance best practice states that ASM follows the rule-based democratic model, with the ASM Twelve Best Practices being the irrevocable constitution, the ASM steering committee being the legislators representing constituents (application users), the ASM custodians being the executive branch, the ASM methodology being the complete set of laws covering all locations and circumstances, and the auditors checking if ASM practitioners are following their own rules being justice. Details describing ASM governance as a democracy are in Appendix F.

For day-to-day operations, ASM governance best practice states that there must be a Master ASM Team Structure which applies equally to every Level Blue application environment. The Master ASM Team Structure is cross-functional and inter-company, with roles and responsibilities approximated as follows:

- *Application Owner,* who uses and owns the application, and in most cases, pays the ASM bills and is responsible, if not for the whole profit center, at least for the value the application provides to the profit center.

- *Application Steering Committee,* whose membership is the representative stakeholders (constituents) using the application, and whose members decide on the ASM work priorities.

- *ASM Solution Manager,*[9] responsible for custodial ASM of the application and following the ASM Twelve Best Practices with rigor and discipline.

- *ASM Custodial Team* of ASM practitioners reporting organizationally to the ASM Solution Manager and supporting, maintaining, and enhancing the application as per priorities set by the application steering committee.

- *Power Users,* who have very strong knowledge on the use of the application and who assist and train others in the use of the application.

- *Help Desk Liaison,*[9] a help desk worker knowledgeable in the application and who is a go-to person for other help desk staff for information about the application.

- *Infrastructure Liaison,*[9] who is an infrastructure worker, not a manager, knowledgeable in the underlying infrastructure used by the application.

- *Production Control Contact,*[9] who is responsible for code integrity of this application.

The concept behind the Master ASM Team Structure is that for every

---

9   These positions could be third-party vendors in outsourcing arrangements.

Level Blue application there must be a corresponding team of workers who are capable of supporting the application in perpetuity without management intervention.

From a strategic viewpoint, ASM governance best practice states that the application service chain (operational) must be aligned to the corporate value chain (strategic) that it services. This means three steering committees, each providing governance to the next, must be established as shown in Figure 13.

FIGURE 13. APPLICATION SERVICE CHAIN GOVERNANCE

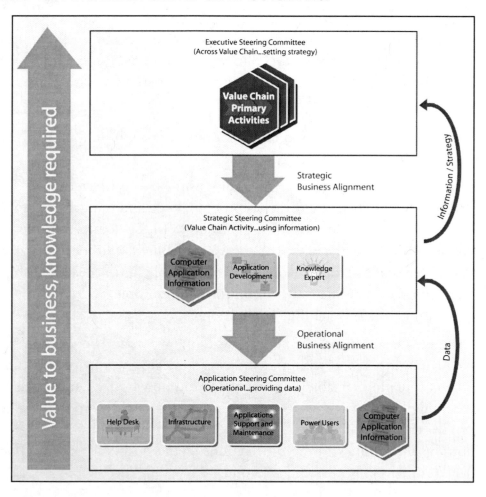

The steering committees are as follows:

- *Executive Steering Committee* provides the highest level business and IT decision making for the information environment. The prime responsibility is the integration of the Line of Business (LOB) plans and objectives with the five-year strategic plan. This includes integrating related business and IT initiatives to maximize business contribution.

- *Strategic Steering Committee* is responsible for investment strategy for the value chain. The committee provides investment criteria to the application steering committee in the form of guiding principles, decision criteria, and portfolio weighing factors.

- *Application Steering Committee* is the operational committee responsible for the governance of the Level Blue applications and the execution of the work in a manner that reflects the investment strategy. This is the committee that manages the ASM custodial team.

There are two steps involved in configuration and setup of an ASM environment for good governance:

Step #1: Obtain enterprise-wide consensus on the Master ASM Team Structure. The structure must be corporate-wide and standardized so that it represents the values of the organization. The structure also must not dilute ASM best practices. For every Level Blue application, assign appropriate staff to create a workgroup responsible for the custodianship of the application. Some staff, liaison roles for example, will have multiple roles on multiple Level Blue applications.

Step #2: Organize and align the application owners and application steering committees to fit within the existing strategic governance structure of the corporation. Enable procedures for top down governance such that each application steering committee can execute the corporate strategy set for their line of business. Align the authority, responsibility, scope and timing of meetings to the expectations of the business first, and to the needs of the ASM custodians second.

Operationally, governance involves the application steering committee executing the following duties:

- Setting work priorities using ordinals and resolving competing work requests/requirements from the business. This is characteristic of ASM environments where there is unlimited demand for service but limited funding to provide the service. The environment must be managed.

- On large enhancements, monitoring progress and controlling scope creep.

- Ensuring the ASM process is followed and only approved prioritized work is done by the custodians.

- Monitoring the ASM custodians and watching for potential issues that may be symptomatic of deeper problems.

All other aspects of ASM governance follow the democratic model as described in Appendix F.

Best Practice #7
Tools

Tools states that ASM-specific computer tools that inherently "encode" the ASM Twelve Best Practices must be utilized by ASM practitioners. As in any discipline, mandatory use of tools helps ensure that practitioners really are following best practices.

In theory, computer applications, being assets, should be manageable using any enterprise asset management tool like Avantis. Help desk tools that track incidents—Remedy being one example—should also be candidates for ASM, as should popular time tracking tools. The challenge is that none of these tool builders recognize ASM as a distinct discipline and strive to digitally encode all ASM Twelve Best Practices. It is only by accident that any of the popular tools encode any of the ASM best practices. Hence, when describing best practice #7, a theoretical ASM-specific tool is used.

Encoding the ASM Twelve Best Practices in ASM-specific tools requires an architecture with two capabilities:

1. *Configuration and Setup*: The ability to capture and store an organization's operating model in a manner that aligns the ASM best practices to the organization's business without diluting the rigor of either.

2. *Operations*: The ability to report on a regular basis, all of the following:

   - *Assets* at multiple management levels (application hierarchy);

   - *Costs* (team of knowledgeable people needed to service the application. A team for an application might consist of ASM programmers, power users, application owner, production control staff, ASM solution manager); reported against each asset.

   - *Value* (activity, work, and accomplishments of the team); reported against each asset.

As part of operations, the architecture must support day to day input of two key documents on which all ASM activity is ultimately measured and managed: tickets and timesheets. These two capabilities are described in the ASM Toolset.

ASM Toolset: Configuration and Setup

The architecture of Configuration and Setup in the ASM Toolset is illustrated in Figure 12. The technical part of the architecture (ASM Taxonomy: Master Taxonomy and Local Configuration) is shown vertically, with unchanging master aspects mainly on the right hand side of the diagram. The business part of the architecture (asset, value, cost, governance) is shown horizontally, under the headings:

- Assets: The Application Portfolio

- Value: The ASM Services

- Costs: The skill-sets needed

- Management: The governance structure

FIGURE 12. ASM CONFIGURATION AND SETUP

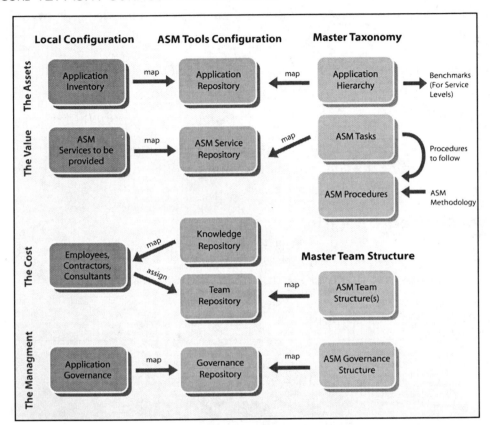

Each of the repositories is described below.

Application Repository, providing a repository of all applications in the corporation organized into Levels Blue, Green and Yellow. All attributes of the applications are stored here. From an executive viewpoint, this is where all the assets and important attributes of those assets are stored.

ASM Service Repository, providing a menu of ASM services, mapped to the master taxonomy's task taxonomy. Linked to each ASM service via the ASM Master Task Taxonomy is the detailed ASM procedure to follow.

Knowledge Repository, representing the IT and business knowledge needed to support the application portfolio. Education, training and certification requirements are captured here. The IT knowledge is organized as per the skill-set hierarchy in the Master Taxonomy. The business knowledge is organized in a business specific framework.

Team Repository, a list of all workers, their associated skill-set and their past, current and potential future assignments to ASM Workgroups as per the ASM team structure.

Governance Repository, containing a record of all major decisions and meetings minutes regarding the application. The minutes of all ASM steering committee meetings are stored here.

ASM Toolset: Operations

The architecture of the operations in the ASM Toolset is shown in Figure 14. Operations best practices are described in the next chapter.

FIGURE 14. ASM OPERATIONS

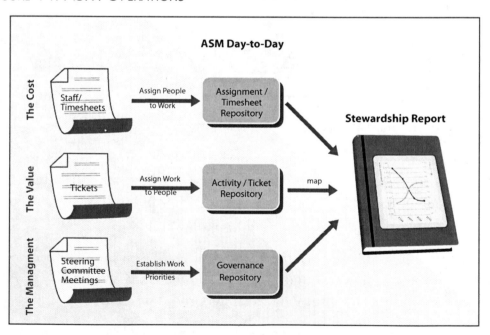

A description of each of the three repositories is shown below.

Assignment/Timesheet Repository, containing a list of trained and capable staff and their current (and past and future) workgroup assignments, with start dates and end dates. It also contains all completed timesheets for purposes of accounting and cost allocation.

Activity/Ticket Respository, containing application documentation descibed in best practice #2.

Governance Repository, containing the decisions and results from each application steering committee meeting: new tickets promoted to "top 10" for work, new tickets backlogged, old backlogged tickets promoted, tickets backdoored (not approved but done anyway), tickets resolved, tickets worked on but still not resolved, and backlogged ticket analysis, as well as agendas and minutes for every meeting. Also contains stewardship reports and other documents associated with ASM governance.

One of the benefits of using ASM-specific tools with best practices digitally encoded is transparency. Management is able to view both the structure and the activity by "walking around" the data repositories. Electronic management by walking around, or e-MBWA, is quickly becoming an essential capability of both the organization, and the management that runs the organization. An example showing how to e-MBWA the ASM-specific tool checking for organizational adherence to the ASM Twelve Best Practices is shown in Appendix B.

Like all tools, ASM-specific tools need regular tuning and maintenance. One needs to be sure that the localized taxonomy is properly adjusted to fit the current business drivers of the ASM environment, and is fine tuned for maximum efficiency and usability of staff. Un-tuned and broken ASM-specific tools cause programmer misalignment, inefficiency, and low morale. They should not be permitted. Retuning of the ASM tools is part of the ASM life cycle best practice described in the next chapter.

TABLE 10. TOOLS SUMMARY

Tools Summary
The ASM Twelve Best Practices digitally codified in the ASM tool to help ensure all staff follow the ASM best practices.
The ASM taxonomy, life cycle, and methodology set up and reflected in the ASM tool.
ASM team structure and individual assignments set up and reflected in the ASM tool.

Note that the ASM tool must be able to list and count everything. Time and cost reporting are left to the accounting discipline using their tools and procedures. More sophisticated IT organizations may want value, time, and money within the ASM discipline. This means the ASM tool must not only support time and cost capability, but must also integrate closely with the accounting discipline's tools and procedures to ensure consistency of information in both disciplines. This integration requirement adds a whole new dimension to the tool requirement.

This completes ASM configuration and setup. The application environment should now be capable of achieving IT operational excellence using ASM best practices #8 to #11 described in the next chapter.

Chapter 4

OPERATIONAL EXCELLENCE: MANAGING IT ASSETS FOR BUSINESS OWNERS

IT operational excellence, rigor and discipline around a centralized ASM process is achievable only if best practices #5 to #8 in configuration and setup were correctly completed. The operational excellence best practices described in this chapter operate based on the single enterprise-wide standard established in the previous chapter. In other words, tickets and timesheets are entered, stored, and reported based on a standardized taxonomy and governance structure established in the previous chapter. The process for tickets and timesheets is centrally managed and controlled by tweaking the configuration and setup parameters described in the previous chapter.

The ASM fundamental principle of ASM ≠ AD is important in this next suite of ASM best practices. Because applications and the associated ASM continue to exist in perpetuity, it follows that the ASM methodology must operate in perpetuity. Thus, every ASM methodology must be inherently cyclic, repeating itself year after year. A circle (or cycle) is the basic mathematical structure for things without beginning or end. The cyclical life cycle of the ASM methodology is fundamental to ASM operations.

Best Practice #8
Cyclical Life Cycle

Cyclical Life Cycle states that every ASM methodology must follow a life cycle whose core is cyclic—a circle without beginning or end. The ASM Cyclical Life Cycle is fundamental to the ASM methodology; it is the cornerstone on which all operational ASM best practices are built, and a keystone on which sits much of the ASM process.

With the mathematical circle being the ASM roadmap, ASM practitioners and their associates, application owners, and senior IT executives must continuously drive all the organization's applications through the predefined application cycle each year. The result is an application that is continuously rejuvenated and constantly aligned to the business environment. The ASM Cyclical Life Cycle, the roadmap to be followed, is shown in Figure 15. See Appendix I, SMART, for detailed reference material on this life cycle.

FIGURE 15. ASM CYCLICAL LIFE CYCLE

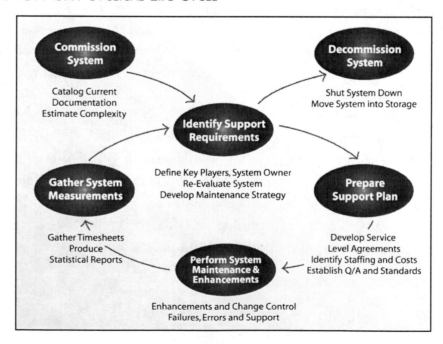

The business equivalent to the ASM Cyclical Life Cycle is shown in Figure 16:

FIGURE 16. STANDARD BUSINESS CYCLE

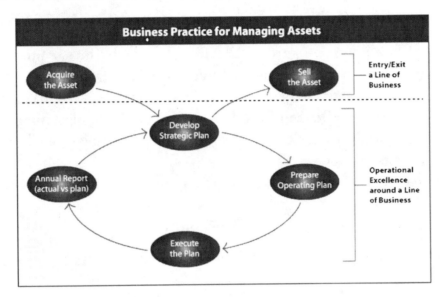

The ASM Cyclical Life Cycle is complete in its description of an application. It shows the application being created in the commission system bubble, entering the circle of life defined by the four bubbles located in the center and connected to form a circle, following that circle of life (more accurately reflected as a bio-rhythm in this context) repeatedly on an annual basis, and then exiting the circle of life to the decommission system bubble.

Hence, as described in the ASM Cyclical Life Cycle, an application starts life with commission system and lives life by following a repeated annual bio-rhythm of four main cycles...

Cycle #1: Identify support requirements,

Cycle #2: Prepare support plan,

Cycle #3: Perform system maintenance and enhancement,

Cycle #4: Gather system measurements,

…and then ends life with decommission system.

The four ASM cycles are described below. The equivalent business process is bracketed.

Cycle #1: Identify Support Requirements (Strategic Plan)

In ASM, "identify support requirements," is the business equivalent of, and an important part of, the annual business planning process, where the corporation's strategy is established for the next several years. In that sense the "identify support requirements" cycle is the "build the application strategy" part of the ASM life cycle. It generates the guiding principles for all ASM activity for the next several years.

The activity of identifying support requirements must occur in the same timeframe as the corporate strategic planning process, but be subservient and subsequent to it. It involves three distinct processes, described below.

Process #1: Define Key Players, System Owner – ie. establish ASM governance.

IT does not own the computer applications; business users do. IT and IT staff are the custodians of the applications. The "define key players, system owners" process establishes (and reconfirms each year) ASM governance principles around ownership and custodianship. The application owner and key stakeholders identified here (aka the application steering committee) define the governance structure for the application asset, whereby business owners set direction and establish priorities for IT custodians. The process also establishes the governance linkage to the executive steering committee described in best practice #6, governance. The primary role of the application steering committee is execution of higher-level strategies while at the same time ensuring continued reliable, usable, low-cost applications are available for the line of business. This paradigm of application ownership/custodianship and governance linkage to the corporate value chain is crucial to creating a successful ASM environment.

Process #2: Re-Evaluate System – ie. align to the business.

Aligning the application inventory and ASM services to the corporate investment strategy each year is important. In terms of aligning the application inventory, the application hierarchy is not usually impacted by the corporate strategic plan. The Level Blue applications (the business functions) rarely change unless there is significant business change. The Level Green applications (the commonly known applications) can sometimes be revamped or replaced to take advantage of new technology defined in the corporate strategic plan. The Level Yellow applications (the program modules) are constantly being replaced and changed by the ASM custodians to allow for changed/enhanced features required in the applications, but this is not detailed in the corporate strategic plan.

In terms of aligning ASM services, the corporate strategic plan often has impact. ASM services can be added, changed or deleted to reflect realities in the business environment. For example, during tough economic times, or for an application being replaced in the near future, a company may decide to strategically stop all enhancement work. Enhancement would no longer be an available ASM service.

Process #3: Develop Maintenance Strategy – ie. application specific strategy.

Application custodians do not design strategies; application owners do. Hence the application owners, not IT, must own and drive the ASM maintenance strategy for each application. ASM custodians participate and assist in the preparation of the maintenance strategy by providing to application owners information and metrics from the ASM stewardship report and data repositories. The application steering committee is responsible for ensuring that the application strategy aligns to the business and investment strategy generated by the executive steering committee.

Examples of some possible strategies are shown in Table 11:

TABLE 11. EXAMPLES OF ASM STRATEGIES

Zero Cost Strategy	No functionality changes No hardware changes No operating system upgrades Replace application every 2 – 5 years Get around failures and inadequacies manually All support done by user or by the package vendor example. PC software packages
Minimal Cost Strategy	No functionality changes No upgrades for new hardware or operating systems Fix failures and perform mandatory changes only Minimal support for users example. Application which is targeted for replacement in the near future
Normal ASM Strategy	Perform mandatory changes Evolve functionality to create a better application via prioritized enhancements Upgrade technology platform of software as per corporate technology strategy Fix failures and the cause of failures. Reduce number of failures and problems occurring Provide Strong user support Example. Most in-house developed software should fall under this option.
Software Evolution Strategy	Target the application for a major upgrade Create major project with project manager to run the upgrade Install upgrade without any outage Invoke extra user support after upgrade to resolve expected bugs Example. New version release of existing application
Software Re-Engineering Strategy	Modify internal program and/or its data structure without altering its functionality Re-structure code Candidate for offshore work example Conversion from Cobol Mainframe to Linux Java.
Software re-development Strategy	Create separate development project outside Custodians to build or buy new software Allow custodians to continue maintaining the old application while developers build new application un-impeded by the maintenance requirements

Cycle #2: Prepare Support Plan (Operating Plan)

A detailed ASM support plan is generated for each Level Blue application committing to headcount, budgets, and operational targets for the next year. This plan, called a support plan, is a subset, and feeds into the IT operating plan for IT and/or the line of business operating plan.

The ASM support plan represents the ASM custodians' commitments to the application owners for the next year, which in some cases becomes part of the formal legal contract for ASM services for the application. The legal contracts are called service levels and are described later in this chapter. The plan is created based on the ASM requirements established in Cycle #1. There are three processes involved in generating the support plan:

Process #1: Develop Service Level Agreements

This process defines the measurable goals by which management will monitor progress towards the strategic goals already set. Normally the goals are target performance levels for the application itself (e.g. reliable, available, useful, user friendly) and/or the ASM service around the application (time to respond to an incident, time to resolve a problem, cost of the service). The goals are often based on the metrics described later in this chapter. If the ASM service is in-sourced, the more general management term Key Performance Indicators (KPI's) may make more sense. Service Level Agreements is a widely used term in IT outsourcing agreements. Irrespective of the terminology used, process #1 is the development of measurable goals that align to the application strategy against which management is measured and sometimes remunerated.

Process #2: Identify Staffing and Costs

Costs associated with ASM are almost exclusively a function of headcount—no other cost components are significant in ASM cost calculations. Since headcount is totally variable from a corporate perspective, the ability to accurately estimate required headcount based on required ASM services and service levels, generated in process #1 above, is a competency that must be core to the ASM custodian. Furthermore, the ASM custodian is expected to treat these estimates as professional commitments and deliver the value promised (ASM services and service levels) for the cost (headcount) committed. Meeting numbers and enabling flexibility in ASM is important to executives managing a line of business. For example, the ability to increase/decrease the cost/value as directed by the application steering committee reflects realities in day to day business.

Process #3: Establish Q/A and Standards

Quality assurance (Q/A) and standards—making sure the ASM Twelve Best Practices and other corporate best practices are being followed—involves updating information, documentation, procedures, and parameter information in the ASM tools, the associated infrastructure tools, and other repositories of information, to reflect the results of the above process; and then following up and ensuring that these tools and the information is used.

Cycle #3: Perform System Maintenance and Enhancements (Execute)

Execution of the support plan and meeting the numbers quoted therein is easy to say but hard to accomplish. That, plus continuous improvement to make applications more reliable, more useful, and less costly, is what cycle #3, perform system maintenance and enhancements, is all about.

Cycle #4: Gather System Measurements (Annual Report to Shareholders)

The importance of Cycle #4 in the ASM cyclical life cycle should never be underestimated or ignored. As any manager will tell you, meeting numbers in the operating plan (Support Plan for ASM) is all-important. Furthermore, being able to drill down and analyze why support plan numbers are not being met (and this will always happen), so corrective action can be recommended, is crucial. It is part of sound business management. ASM is no exception.

Good metrics are also the basis for the feedback mechanism required for the continuous improvement activity described in best practice #10. Metrics help build ASM morale in what otherwise can be quite a mundane environment, as described in best practice #11, benchmarks and service levels.

Best Practice #9
Stewardship Reporting

Stewardship Reporting is about providing unparalleled transparency and accountability to application owners and executives. It is also about celebrating accomplishments of the ASM staff—a rare event in many ASM environments.

From a celebration context, stewardship reporting can be viewed as the apex of the ASM discipline. Like the Olympic Games for athletes, or the Academy Awards for actors, or the Annual/Quarterly Report for CEO's, Best Practice #9: Stewardship Reporting is the annual/quarterly opportunity for ASM professionals to take pride in their profession and to show off to the corporation—or even the world—the results of their work. "See and be seen," "compare and be compared": stewardship reporting can be viewed as publishing metrics for staff motivation.

Formally, stewardship reporting is about ASM custodians showing transparency and accountability to the application owners. The purpose is to present the results of their custodianship tenure, comparing the actual results from the ASM tool to the planned results in the support plan. The stewardship report is similar to the CEO's annual/quarterly report to the shareholders, where actual numbers are compared against plan. The difference is that the CEO is reporting income and balance sheet numbers against plan based on generally accepted accounting principles (GAAP), whereas the ASM custodian is reporting staff headcount, costs, application inventory, ASM service activity, and service levels: actual numbers against planned numbers. For purposes of GAAP comparison, application inventory represents assets, ASM service activity and benchmarks represent revenue (or value), and ASM staff headcount represent costs. Profit (loss) is value minus cost.

TABLE 12. STEWARDSHIP REPORT VS CORPORATE ANNUAL REPORT COMPARISON

Corporate Annual/ Quarterly Report	ASM Stewardship Report Equivalent
GAAP Income Statement and Balance Sheet	Application Inventory (Assets), Custodial Headcount (Costs), and Custodial Activity (Value which equates to Revenue)
Historical Accounting Statements (Revenue, Costs, Balance Sheet items)	Historical Trends, Application Inventory, Custodial Headcount, Custodial Activity
Actual versus Operating Plan – Revenue, Costs.	Actual versus Objectives with respect to headcount, and ticket activity.

The format of the stewardship report, like the corporate annual report, is restrictive in that certain information must be shown, but it is open in terms of presentation style. First, being a report for management, the stewardship report must describe the application's strategic and operating plans in business terminology. It must show last year: plan versus actual; and next year: plan only. Interim quarterly reporting is always against plan. All plan information should follow the format of the Cyclical Life Cycle best practice where Identify Support Requirements is the application's strategic plan, and Prepare Support Plan is the application's operating plan.

Application data that must be reported is described below. All data must be reported primarily against the taxonomy Local Configuration, plus against the Master Taxonomy if comparison to other companies is desirable.

The data reported is as follows:

The Assets: Computer Application Inventory

The stewardship report is yearly compilation of the application inventory of the corporation organized as per the master application taxonomy. The stewardship report is organized with a separate section for each Level Blue application representing either a line of businesses, profit center, or significant business function. This aligns the stewardship report's structure to the business. The technical view (Level Green and Level Yellow applications) is reported under their Level Blue sections as per the application hierarchy.

The People: Custodians of the Assets

Application custodians (headcount, expertise, and responsibility) described in the stewardship report represent the cost of maintaining each Level Blue application. The actual dollars (salaries) are confidential and not normally included, but individual names and their respective expertise and experience are included. Dollars may be included at aggregate levels.

Also included are external people who are part of the application service chain described in the best practices on governance. Application owners, key stakeholders, steering committee members, power users, production control contacts, help desk, and infrastructure liaisons are examples of people who may be part of the application service chain. The stewardship report must document the application service chain team structure showing roles and responsibilities, as well as describe the individuals filling those roles.

The Activity: The Value of Application Custodianship

All ASM activity is recorded in timesheets (how people are assigned to work) and tickets (how work is assigned to people). Stewardship reporting of activity is primarily ticket counts and head counts based on the taxonomy showing inherent characteristics of the underlying applications. The activity is formatted as follows:

- Plan from last year versus actual data

- Plan for next year

Since ticket activity represents ASM value, it is normally the most scrutinized part of the stewardship report.

The stewardship report is not simply dry statistics. Numbers must be interpreted and used to plan and execute next year's strategy. They should enable ASM predictability and repeatability—the "if we do this, we will get that" continuous improvement approach to management. The stewardship report is also an opportunity to demonstrate ASM leadership. Typical questions that should be asked and answered, either directly or woven into the fabric of the report, are:

- What is the corporate business strategy?

- Is the stewardship report aligned?

- What is the hardware and infrastructure strategy? Do they have plans that might impact the application?

- Describe the "competitive" landscape. What do similar companies use for the same Level Blue applications and how do their custodianship costs compare? Are there new technologies or software packages they are using that should be evaluated?

- What is happening in the ASM service provider market? Are there new players with new methodologies, tools, or services?

- What is happening in the ASM community at large?

- Is the market tight for people?

- Is there any way we should be contributing to the ASM community at large?

- What are the sourcing alternatives for ASM?

- Should insourcing, outsourcing, offshoring, or nearshoring be considered?

- Is there a new source of industry benchmarks (other than our own history) that we can compare to?

Best Practice #10
Continuous Improvement Culture

Continuous Improvement Culture is the second of two ASM cultural best practices. It is an extension of Best Practice #3: Problem Ownership Culture. Both instill a burning drive in every ASM practitioner to remove every single problem from every single application on the planet.

Continuous Improvement, however, brings predictability and repeatability to the discipline.

> Continuous improvement culture is:
>
> 1. increase reliability
>
> 2. increase usability
>
> 3. decrease costs
>
> Until customers are delivered predictable, smooth-running applications with minimal support costs.

Continuous Improvement Culture is an extension of Problem Ownership Culture in that:

- Continuous Improvement uses ASM metrics to plan, measure and report progress year over year, whereas Problem Ownership depends on encouragement and anecdotal evidence. Continuous improvement depends on rigor and discipline around the stewardship reporting best practice; problem ownership does not.

- Continuous Improvement is a managed activity, where ASM managers plan, organize, predict, and then commit to improvements based on their understanding of historical data. Continuous Improvement is characterized by "if we do this," (e.g. change something), "then we will get that" (e.g. reduce failures). This approach differs from the problem ownership culture, where there is total dependence on individual professionalism. This is what introduces predictability and repeatability to the ASM discipline.

- Continuous Improvement is a process that integrates into the Cyclical Life Cycle (best practice #8), and Stewardship Reporting (best practice #9) as part of the planning and reporting process. Problem Ownership does not.

- Rewards are based on metrics, not intuition.

When ASM is totally integrated into the application service chain, which is in turn integrated into the corporate value chain to provide end-to-end service, continuous improvement can be again extended. These initiatives must be driven by the business executive as part of the business value chain.

Two continuous improvement extensions come into play when ASM participates in an end-to-end continuous improvement business initiative.

1. There is the scientific aspect of continuous improvement, based on statistical process control (SPC) processes developed by Dr W. Edwards Deming[10]. The key to success in using the SPC process is identifying meaningful data describing the end-to-end process. While not cost effective by itself in ASM, participating in an end-to-end SPC initiative that includes the whole application service chain is beneficial. The essence of SPC is that ticket data can be analyzed statistically to accurately predict the future and this future can be predictably altered by changing some aspect of the process.

2. There is the extension of continuous improvement concepts to all people in all disciplines in every link in both the application service chain and the associated value chain, such that the Japanese principle of *kaizen* can be implemented. The essence of *kaizen* is the notion that all disciplines in the service chain, and their managers, practitioners and workers, collaborate continually to systemize the service tasks and to identify incremental changes, all with the goal of making the end service run more smoothly. For example, *kaizen* from an application perspective means continual collaboration between ASM, infrastructure, help desk, application users, and application knowledge experts, to improve the application.

Best practice #10 is summarized in Table 13:

---

10 The Deming Management Method, Mary J. Walton, Perigree Books, 1986.
Building Continual Improvement, A Guide for Business, Donald J. Wheeler and Sheila R Poling, SPC Press 1998.

TABLE 13. SML IMPLEMENTATION GUIDELINES FOR ASM BEST PRACTICE #10

Continuous Improvement Culture Summary

Capability to measure and report on the results of the intrinsic desire to remove problems and fix errors so the number of issues is reduced. Continuous improvement is implemented via consistent, careful and accurate measurement of appropriate counts and then rewarding people when they improve the reliability, usability and cost-effectiveness of an application.

Introduces predictability and repeatability to ASM.

Best Practice #11
Benchmarks and Service Levels

ASM benchmarks, by definition of the word benchmark, are industry standard metrics that all ASM service providers (including in-house ASM organizations) publish and use for ASM performance comparison. To be benchmarks, they must be accurate and ubiquitous. To be used, they must be simple, easy to understand, easy to measure, and easily available…like the price/earnings ratio of the stock market.

ASM Service Levels (often referred to as Service Level Agreements, or SLA's) are legally binding contracts between an ASM service provider and an application owner regarding details of the ASM services being provided. They are specific to a service and to a service provider/owner agreement and are therefore not benchmarks—although both benchmarks and SLA's can be based on the same metric. SLA's are created to align IT's goals to the business objectives and business strategy. They are the IT equivalent to the Key Performance Indicators (KPI's) used in normal business management.

The Benchmarks and Service Levels are used for two reasons:

1. To enable ASM management by metrics as normally characterized by SLA's or KPI's.

2.   To hire and inspire staff to be best in class in ASM as normally character-
     ized by benchmarks.

ASM, being a new discipline, has no established metrics for either benchmarks or SLA's. Thus, creating meaningful metrics for benchmarks or SLA's
can be a daunting task, even for sophisticated organizations. Using new, un-
proven metrics as contractual SLA's runs the risk of providing unexpected
and even negative results to the corporation. For example, the metric "IT cost
as a percentage of revenue" may not be a good SLA in some organizations.
As mentioned in Chapter One, both best performing and worst performing
companies spend less than average on IT, and there is no statistical correlation. Hence, introducing an "IT cost as a percentage of revenue" KPI to the
wrong organization is risky. The process of identifying SLA's that align to the
corporate strategy is inherent in the ASM cyclical life cycle. Again, adopting
vendor SLA's or SLA's from other companies without following the internal
consideration of fit is extremely risky.

Cleary, if universal benchmarks were established and reliable for ASM,
organizations would prefer to use these industry benchmarks for SLA's with
minor adjustments to fit organizational requirements. Inasmuch as ASM is
the new IT discipline, however, there are no established, reliable, and standard
metrics. But there are several ASM metrics currently used that may evolve in
standards.

Two types of metrics are gathered in ASM: metrics about the application
itself, and metrics about the service provided by the application custodian.
Metrics about the application itself are:

- Availability
- Usability
- Reliability
- Organizational value
- Ease of use
- Total cost of ownership

While metrics about the application itself are highly valued by executive management, the lack of consistency among business and application environments means these metrics lack ubiquity and are open to interpretation as to what is good and what is bad. Hence they are mainly restricted to internal use, comparing this year to last year, looking for trends.

Universal metrics measuring the effectiveness of the ASM service provider are more conducive to benchmarking.

- Time to respond

- Time to resolve

These two metrics can be utilized across the entire application portfolio of any organization, current and future, using the application importance attribute and the task taxonomy from the ASM Master Taxonomy. An example is given in Appendix C.

As a profession and a new discipline, ASM must push to evolve metrics that can be utilized as both benchmarks and KPI's. A good example is the Olympics. Olympic organizers have created an environment where the absolute best world-wide work their hearts out and compete tirelessly for the opportunity to participate. There is no other environment where multi-million dollar celebrities beg to be allowed to participate for free. It bears repeating from Chapter One: Olympic metrics have five attributes that make them stand out. They are immediate, accurate, final, international, and consistent—and worthy of emulation.

Creating an environment where the absolute best beg to be allowed to compete...the Olympics... is the environment this ASM best practice should aspire to emulate.

Operational excellence in ASM, the flawless execution of the just described eleven best practices, brings reliable, useful, low-cost applications to end users. And they bring security, integrity, reliability, and predictability into the whole IT environment. Operational excellence in IT is an approach that should not—indeed, must not—be ignored by the executive of a corporation.

However, it must also be recognized that IT organizations are all different.

Different sizes, different corporate cultures, different maturity levels, and different operating models all impact the way the above ASM eleven best practices are implemented. The twelfth ASM best practice, ASM Maturity Levels, and the final chapter, Self Assessment, show how to implement and optimize the ASM twelve best practices in an IT organization.

Chapter 5

SELF-ASSESSMENT: OPTIMIZING ASM BEST PRACTICES TO YOUR ORGANIZATION

ASM self-assessment involves first understanding which of three underlying value disciplines the IT organization ascribes to:

1. Product leadership

2. Customer intimacy

3. Operational excellence

and then assessing the ASM maturity level for an appropriate fit.

IT Value Discipline Self-Assessment

As mentioned, while it is important to strive for excellence in all three value disciplines, one must be chosen as prime to drive decisions, resolve conflicts, and set priorities[11]. Following, are the inherent characteristics of each value discipline as it relates to IT.

Operational Excellence

- The primary role of IT is ASM. AD is secondary. IT is viewed as a commodity having no potential for competitive advantage in the organization.

---

11 Treacy and Wiersema, "The Discipline of Market Leadership",

- Most of the computer applications are either legacy in-house developed software or newly purchased packages. There is very little ongoing custom development of new applications.

- IT is organized such that it can be viewed as a series of IT application service chains linked to the organization's profit centers. These end-to-end service chains are optimized and streamlined to minimize costs and hassle.

- Application custodianship (ASM) with respect to the IT application service chains is clearly differentiated from AD. The role for AD is looking for cheaper/better/faster sub-components of the IT application service chain under the direction of the profit center.

- The process around the IT application service chain is centralized and tightly controlled. Discipline (methodology, tools, people certification), governance, process, ASM structure, and budget are centralized.

- Democracy is the primary governance model for work prioritization.

Product Leadership

- ASM is organizationally indistinguishable from AD; ASM is an adjunct to the AD team charged with looking after all lines of business, profit centers, and significant business functions and/or ASM is organizationally separate from AD but is the back end of a "Plan/Build/ Operate" way of thinking.

- ASM work is differentiated from AD work mainly at the ticket level by using an arbitrary level of effort, dollars, or time to decide which is which.

- IT managers are constantly scrambling for capital project dollars and promoting new project ideas in an effort to keep their teams intact. This puts huge internal pressure on the organization to be creative with respect to new IT projects.

- AD capital depreciation is pooled and not viewed as an ongoing expense to the line of business and/or application custodians. Bottom line accountability for AD cost is less important than retaining product leadership. AD is considered a cost of doing business.

Customer Intimacy

- IT is organizationally dispersed into the company's lines of business, profit centers and/or significant business functions. This dispersion can be physical with programmers reporting to the business units, or it can be structural with budget, decision-making, and process being controlled by the business units, irrespective of where the pool of programmers resides.

ASM Maturity Levels (SML) Self Assessment

Self-assessment regarding the internal usage of the ASM Twelve Best Practices is not helpful unless the value discipline and underlying operating model for IT, both current and future, are clarified. Depending on the operating model selected—product leadership, customer intimacy, or operational excellence—and depending on the size and sophistication of the IT organization, different ASM maturity levels (SML) should be implemented in the organization.

For IT organizations not pursuing operational excellence, or for small IT organizations, the ASM basics (best practices #1 to #4) should be implemented. For IT organizations pursuing operational excellence as the primary value discipline, then first ASM Configuration and Setup (best practices #5 to #7) need to be completed, and subsequently ASM Operational Excellence (best practices #8 to #11) can be implemented. For still other IT organizations that fall in between these two extremes, there are other ASM implementation options using ASM Maturity Levels as shown in Table 14.

TABLE 14. ASM BEST PRACTICES IMPLEMENTED WITHIN ASM MATURITY LEVELS

ASM Maturity Level	ASM Best Practice
Level 1: Team Fiefdoms Independent focus on keeping the customer happy.	1. Change Control, Security, and Integrity 2. Documentation
Level 2: Process Identification ASM is organizationally recognized as a separate entity distinct from AD and infrastructure.	3. Problem Ownership Culture 4. Black Box Delivery Model
Level 3: Process Utilization ASM is a formal discipline with one automated standardized ASM process for measuring/ reporting ASM size (application inventory), activity (tasks) and governance (priorities) for the whole organization.	5. Taxonomy 6. Governance 7. Tools 8. Cyclical Life Cycle 9. Stewardship Reporting 10. Continuous Improvement Culture
Level 4: Best Practices ASM process improvement is measured in time and value as opposed to counts and activity	11. Benchmarks and Service Levels 12. ASM maturity levels
Level 5: Transparency ASM is an integrated link in the Application Service Chain where ASM cost, value, and time are managed as subunits of the end service or product being delivered.	

Some organizations with a management culture of process management and control (a large multinational bank) will want the ASM best practices implemented with a high level of ASM maturity. Other organizations with a culture of decentralized control and minimal implementation of management process (a group of university professors) will want the ASM best practices implemented with a low level of ASM maturity. The diagram in Figure 17 shows best practice implementation of the ASM maturity levels based on the size of the IT organization and the corporate culture around process management.

Figure 17. ASM Maturity Levels Implementation

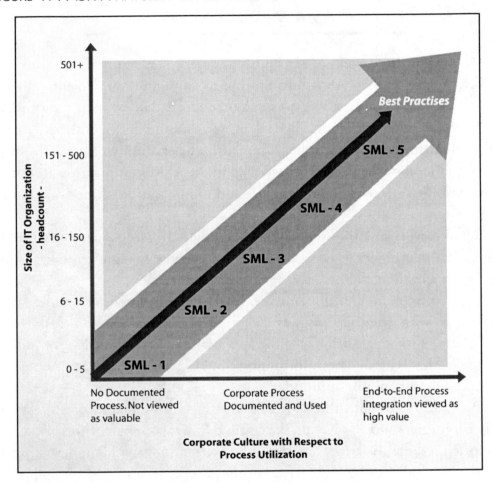

The ASM maturity levels are formally described in the last best practice below with details in Appendices D and E.

Best Practice #12
ASM Maturity Levels

ASM Maturity Levels (SML) is an assessment (a measurement if you like) of the capability of an ASM organization to configure, implement, and follow the ASM Twelve Best Practices in a manner that aligns with and provides relevance to the corporation. SML does not measure assets, activity, cost, or value of an application portfolio. It measures the capability of the ASM organization to follow the processes described in the ASM best practices in a manner that is cost effective and fits the size and sophistication of the organization it serves.

Unlike other maturity models, such as CMMI[12] (see Appendix D), SML recognizes that higher levels of SML do not necessarily represent better value to the organization.

For example, in a small company, SML-1, represented by a super smart individual with extensive business and application knowledge, available on a 24/7 basis working alone to keep the application users happy, is a formidable efficiency that is hard to beat. Introducing SML-3 with its associated costs and overheads would not be appropriate.

As another example, the value of matching culture in a business relationship is nothing short of pivotal. The cultural fit between partner organizations can often serve as the critical success or failure point of any IT undertaking. In ASM, this could not be more true. For the success of our ASM discipline, we all must work to instill the cultural aspect of reducing problems. This can be done at either the problem ownership level of maturity or at the continuous improvement level of maturity. Introducing continuous improvement culture to an organization that neither practices it nor sees its value may be a detraction rather than an added value. These organizations may be better off staying at SML-3 or lower.

Hence the importance of matching ASM process maturity (SML) to the

---

12   Capability Maturity Model created by the Software Engineering Institute (SEI) at Carnegie Mellon University

corporate organizational maturity. A good indicator of which ASM maturity level is the best fit is size of IT organization. Figure 18 graphs size of organization against SML, and shows the best-fit SML. The bottom right triangle describes companies that have invested too much money and management time in ASM processes, and are at an SML above where they should be. As a result, these organizations are top heavy, expending too much money managing too little work. On the other end of the spectrum is the top left triangle. In this quadrant, given the size, complexity, and importance of the application environment, these companies' ASM management and depth of ASM process is too thin. These companies are bottom heavy with out-of-control ASM expenditures (too high or too low) thereby risking catastrophic application failure.

FIGURE 18. ASM MATURITY LEVELS BEST FIT

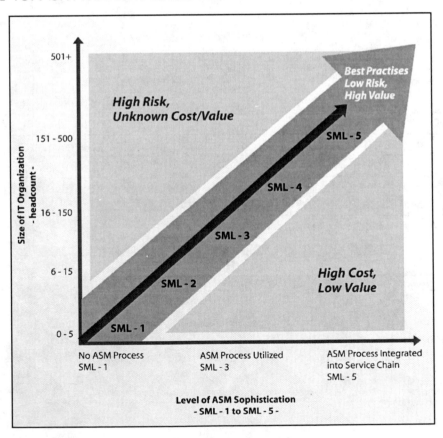

Introducing the right subset of the ASM Twelve Best Practices at the right moment of time in a growing organization is key to successful ASM. SML-3 is where "real" ASM begins, and is what most organizations should strive to attain initially. The table below summarizes the ASM Twelve Best Practices and shows where they should be introduced as an organization grows in size and dependency on its applications.

TABLE 15. INTRODUCING ASM BEST PRACTICES AT THE APPROPRIATE ASM MATURITY LEVEL

Best Practice	SML-1	SML-2	SML-3	SML-4	SML-5
1. Change Control, Security, and Integrity	Initiate	Enhance	Enhance	Continue	Continue
2. Documentation	Initiate	Enhance	Enhance	Continue	Continue
3. Problem Ownership Culture		Initiate	Continue	Continue	Continue
4. Black Box Delivery Model		Initiate	Continue	Continue	Continue
5. Taxonomy			Initiate	Continue	Continue
6. Governance			Initiate	Continue	Continue
7. Tools			Initiate	Continue	Continue
8. Cyclical Life Cycle			Initiate	Continue	Continue
9. Stewardship Reporting			Initiate	Continue	Continue
10. Continuous Improvement Culture			Initiate	Continue	Enhance
11. Benchmarks and Service Levels				Initiate	Enhance
12. ASM Maturity Levels				Initiate	Continue

"Initiate" means that this best practice is introduced for the first time at this SML. Lower SML's do not have this best practice

"Enhance" means this best practice, while implemented at lower SML's is more comprehensive and needs expansion at this SML

"Continue" means this best practice is identical at this SML to the implementation at the lower SML.

" " <blank> means this best practice is not implemented or used at this SML.

The ASM maturity levels and the ASM Twelve Best Practices implemented at each of those levels is described in Appendix E. An ASM Maturity Level assessment matrix is in Appendix G.

This concludes the ASM Twelve Best Practices—and this book. For some, the book will appear to have been a simple reiteration of common sense. For others, the same words will be heresy. My hope is that I have shed some new light on this seemingly nebulous profession called IT, and that whatever your future decision is with respect to IT, it provides a lasting competitive advantage – both personally and corporately.

Appendix A

ASM Master Taxonomy

Taxonomy	Taxonomy - Level 1	Taxonomy - Level 2	Definition and Description
Application Taxonomy	Application Hierarchy	Application Inventory viewed at: • Level Blue • Level Green • Level Yellow	Level Blue: profit center, line of business or significant business function. Level Green: common acronym/name used by business staff when submitting tickets. Level Yellow: names for modules, programs, code-components relevant to technical staff.
	Application Importance	• Mission Critical • Critical • Vital • Important	Mission Critical: If the application is down for more than a few hours, then normal business stops. Impact is risk of business failure. Critical: If the application is down for more than a few days, then normal business stops. Impact is risk of business failure. Vital: if the application fails, business can carry on for several weeks but with several disruption and risk of business damage. Important: If the application fails then business can carry on indefinitely but with severe inconvenience and high additional cost.
	Skill-set Hierarchy	Level 1 - Era • Mainframe • Client Server • Web • Package Specific Level 2 – Vendor Level 3 - Technology	Mainframe: applications running on IBM mainframe, AS400, using Cobol, DB2, IMS – 1970's technology. Client Server: applications running on Wintel, Unix platforms using VB, Oracle or desktop software – 1990's technology. Web: applications on remote servers accessed exclusively via the public internet. Package Specific: Internal support restricted to installing new releases, changing package parameters, answering questions, working with package vendor.
Task Taxonomy	Task Type	• Problem • Enhancement • Data Fix • Information Request	Problem: Coding/data changes needed to make an Application work correctly. Enhancement: New functionality or technology change required of the application. Data Fix: Data changes, data extracts, service pack upgrades using tools too complex for end user computing. Information Request: Investigations, cost/time estimates and questions where no coding or data change is involved.

	Task Lifecycle	• Received • Responded • Resolved	Received: Ticket has been received by Application Custodian. Responded: Custodian has analyzed the ticket and corresponded with the ticket originator about what will be done. Resolved: Ticket is completed to originator's satisfaction.
	Task Priority	• Critical • High • Normal	Critical: Task must be done immediately. Normal processes are circumvented. High: Task must be done immediately but normal processes must be followed. Normal: Most tasks are normal
	Task Value	• Good work • Bad work	Good Work: Work which is planned, organized and executed as per the IT Investment Strategy – normally enhancements. Bad Work: Work which is unplanned, unpredictable, and often disruptive – normally problems.
	Task Occurrence	• Business hours • After hours	Business Hours: task handled within normal working hours. After Hours: Task requires after hours work.
Procedures Taxonomy	Change Procedure	• Emergency change • Normal change	Emergency Change: Procedure to follow when there is insufficient time to follow normal procedures. Normal Change: Normal change procedure to follow.
	Support Process	• Outage • Critical Problem • Normal Request • Quick Fix • Prioritization	Outage: Process to follow when an application is down everywhere and not working for anyone. Critical Problem: Process to follow when an application error is causing major disruptions. Normal Request: Default process to follow. Used for most requests. Quick Fix: Fix immediately while they wait on the phone type process. Used for Data Fixes and Information Requests. Prioritization: Process to follow for non-critical requests that will take a long time or a lot of resources.
	Enhancement Procedure	• ASM responsibility • AD responsibility	ASM: follow ASM procedures. AD: transition application from ASM to AD, follow AD discipline's methodology, transition application from AD back to ASM.
	Transition Process	• From AD to ASM • From one service provider to another	

Appendix B

e-MBWA[13] Example

The ASM Twelve Best Practices	ASM best practices cross check and adherence indicators
1. Change Control, Security, and Integrity	Check that the ASM Master Team Structure crosses functional boundaries in that program changes, final testing, and production control are done by separate people in separate departments.
2. Documentation	Do a count of tickets by Level Blue Applications. All Level Blue Applications should show some ticket activity.
3. Problem Ownership Culture	Create a report of Critical Problem tickets having the longest resolve time over the past year. Talk to the ASM practitioner shown on the ticket as being responsible.
4. Black Box Delivery Model	Review personnel assigned to Workgroups. Does each Workgroup represent a Level Blue Application and does this group account for all application changes?
5. Taxonomy	Enter a ticket and follow the taxonomy choices on the input screen. Are they simple and would they make sense to an average employee?
6. Governance	Get a list of application owners. Do you know and trust them? Email them. Are they aware of their responsibilities?
7. Tools	Create trend graphs for headcount by workgroup (cost) and tickets by application importance (value). Do the cost/value trends match the corporate strategy?
8. Cyclical Life Cycle	Find the Strategic Plan and Operating Plan for the Level Blue applications. Are managers meeting their commitments?

---

13 Management by walking around (MBWA) was described in Tom Peter's classic book *In Search of Excellence*. MBWA is a management technique that involves walking around in the front lines of the business to gather information and obtain insights from front line employees, rather than depending solely on the normal business hierarchy. eMWBA is an electronic version of this technique using information in corporate databases to gain the same insights.

9. Stewardship Reporting	Thumb through a couple of recent Stewardship reports. Send accolade emails to appropriate ASM staff based on metrics reported.
10. Continuous Improvement Culture	Get a series of graphs based on ticket counts. Question staff on the trends. Are they able to accurately predict the future in "if we do this, we will get that"?
11. Benchmarks and Service Levels	Check the average time to resolve critical problems on mission critical applications. How does it compare to industry leaders?
12. ASM Maturity Levels	Do a self-assessment on the ASM maturity level of your ASM organization using Appendix G.

Appendix C

ASM Benchmark Example

Application Importance	Local Configuration Example	Benchmark
Mission Critical If the application is down for more than a few hours, then normal business stops. Impact is risk of business failure.	Problem Critical	Respond = 1 "Hours" Resolve = 2 "Hours"
	Problem High	Respond = 1 "Hours" Resolve = 4 "Hours"
	Problem Normal	Respond = 3 "Support Hours" Resolve = 8 "Support Hours"
	Enhancements	Respond = 1 "Days" Resolve = "Set by Application Steering Committee"
	Data Fixes	Respond = 1 "Hour" Resolve = 4 "Hours"
	Information Requests	Respond = 1 "Hour" Resolve = 4 "Hours"
Critical If the application is down for more than a few days, then normal business stops. Impact is risk of business failure.	Problem Critical	Respond = 3 "Hours" Resolve = 6 "Hours"
	Problem High	Respond = 1 "Support Hour" Resolve = 3 "Support Hours"
	Problem Normal	Respond = 3 "Support Hours" Resolve = 8 "Support Hours"
	Enhancements	Respond = 1 "Day" Resolve = "Set by Application Steering Committee"
	Data Fixes	Respond = 3 "Hours" Resolve = 6 "Hours"
	Information Requests	Respond = 1 "Support Hour" Resolve = 3 "Support Hours"

Vital If the application fails, business can carry on for several weeks but with severe disruption and risk of business damage.	Problem Critical	Respond = 3 "Support Hours" Resolve = 1 "Day"
	Problem High	Respond = 8 "Support Hours" Resolve = 3 "Days"
	Problem Normal	Respond = 2 "Days" Resolve = 10 "Days"
	Enhancements	Respond = 10 "Days" Resolve = "Set by Application Steering Committee"
	Data Fixes	Respond = 1 "Day" Resolve = 1 "Day"
	Information Requests	Respond = 3 "Days" Resolve = 3 "Days"
Important If the application fails then business can carry on indefinitely but with great inconvenience and higher cost.	Problem Critical	Respond = 3 "Days" Resolve = 10 "Days"
	Problem High	Respond = 3 "Days" Resolve = 10 "Days"
	Problem Normal	Respond = 3 "Days" Resolve = 10 "Days"
	Enhancements	Respond = 20 "Days" Resolve = "Set by Application Steering Committee"
	Data Fixes	Respond = 3 "Days" Resolve = 3 "Days"
	Information Requests	Respond = 3 "Days" Resolve = 3 "Days"

Appendix D

ASM Maturity Levels (SML) vs. Capability Maturity Model (CMM)

Level	SML	CMM[14]	Generic Maturity Model[15]
0			Non-existent. Complete lack of any recognizable processes. The organization has not even recognized that there is an issue to be addressed.
1	Team Fiefdoms. Independent focus on keeping the customer happy.	Initial. Few processes defined, most done so on ad hoc basis.	Initial. There is evidence that the organization has recognized that the issues exist and need to be addressed. There are, however, no standardized processes; instead there are ad-hoc approaches that tend to be applied on an individual or case-by-case basis. The overall approach to management is disorganized.
2	Process Identification. ASM is organizationally recognized as a separate entity distinct from AD and infrastructure.	Repeatable. Basic project management processes based on past successes.	Repeatable. Processes have developed to the stage that different people undertaking the same task follow similar procedures. There is no formal training or communication of standard procedures and responsibility is left to the individual. There is a high degree of reliance on the knowledge of individuals, and therefore errors are likely.

3	Process Utilization. ASM is a formal discipline with one automated standardized ASM process for measuring/reporting ASM size (application inventory), activity (tasks), and governance (priorities) for the whole organization.	Defined. Process is documented and integrated into company standard.	Defined. Procedures have been standardized and documented and communicated through training. It is, however, left to the individual to follow these processes, and it is unlikely that deviations will be detected. The procedures themselves are not sophisticated but are the formalization of existing practices.
4	Best Practices. ASM is a formal discipline with one automated standardized ASM process for measuring/reporting size, activity, governance; plus time, value and cost for the whole organization.	Managed. Collection of detailed measurements of software process and quality.	Managed. It is possible to monitor and measure compliance with the procedures and to take action where the processes appear not to be working effectively. Processes are under constant improvement and provide good practice. Automation and tools are used in a limited or fragmented way.
5	Transparency. ASM is an integrated link in the service chain (explained in Chapter 2) where ASM cost, value, and time are managed as sub-units of the end service or product being delivered.	Optimized. Continuous improvement added through feedback and experiment.	Optimized. Processes have been refined to a level of best practice, based on the results of continuous improvement and maturity modeling with other organizations. IT is used in an integrated way to automate the workflow, providing tools to improve quality and effectiveness, making the enterprise quick to adapt.

14   Source: Carnegie Mellon Software Engineering Institute, Capability Maturity Model (CMM) on www. wei.cmu.edu at time of printing.

15   Source: COBIT Management Guidelines available from Information Systems Audit and Control Association (ISACA) Bookstore on www.isaca.org at time of printing.

Appendix E

ASM Maturity Levels (SML) Defined

SML-1 Team Fiefdoms
Independent focus on keeping the customer happy.

Each programmer and analyst has an independent focus on keeping his or her users happy. There is no formal process specific to ASM. Other processes may be utilized but are not ASM-specific. An example of such a process would be the salary review process following HR guidelines.

In a SML-1 environment, there is no independent recognition of ASM. Each IT staff member acts independently as their own IT department; sharing duties with peers through holiday rotation, work responsibility rotation, and sick time backup. Thus each programmer is comfortable handling all aspects of IT in their small shop environment: infrastructure, help desk, deskside, ASM, and AD, as the case may be.

ASM Scalability

The SML-1 best practices in ASM are scaled to reflect a very small IT shop where a few people handle everything. Applications are expected to be purchased off the shelf, be simple to install and operate, and be used "as is." ASM is expected to be minimal or non-existent. Some of the ASM best practices listed in SML-1 below are, in a larger scale IT environment, located in infrastructure and therefore are not described in the rest of this book.

ASM Organizational Capability

Organizational ASM capability at SML-1 is, for all intents and purposes, non-existent.

ASM BEST PRACTICES IMPLEMENTED AT SML-1

SML-1 Best Practices	
1. Change Control, Security, and Integrity	(1) Backup Recovery Rule (2) Data Integrity Rule (3) Testing Rule (4) Source Code Integrity Rule In simplistic terms, the IT manager of the small shop should: o Maintain the integrity of the hardware, software, and applications so that it is not destroyed by "stupid mistakes." Keep the production version of application source code and software locked safely away. Keep daily, weekly, or monthly backups of data on tape. Be able to re-create the environment from scratch starting with brand new hardware as if a fire had wiped everything out last night. o Know how to manage change of hardware, software, and applications so there is minimal impact on the users. For example, make changes on Friday evening so there is lots of time to recover if a disaster happens. Have contingency plan about what to do if the change doesn't work. In other words, be able to back the change out.
2. Documentation	The IT manager keeps all IT records, including those normally retained by Infrastructure, in his/her desk drawer: licenses, warrantees, purchase invoices, user guides, and other documents received when hardware and software are purchased. The IT manager also creates a spreadsheet of hardware, software, and applications highlighting the information needed for getting help on each product—phone number, web site, model or license information they need to answer your call. Finally, the passwords, computer names, software naming conventions, and setup conventions for each computer are kept stored safely by the IT manager so any computer can be re-created from scratch.
3. Problem Ownership Culture	n/a
4. Black Box Delivery Model	n/a

5. Taxonomy	n/a
6. Governance	n/a
7. Tools	n/a
8. Cyclical Life Cycle	n/a
9. Stewardship Reporting	n/a
10. Continuous Improvement Culture	n/a
11. Benchmarks and Service Levels	n/a
12. ASM Maturity Levels	n/a

SML-2 Process Identification
ASM is organizationally recognized as a separate entity distinct from AD and infrastructure.

The premise, and a key difference in reaching SML-2, is that ASM is a distinct group separate from AD and infrastructure. The IT organization is now big enough to merit three separate teams (two if there is no development), each with their own manager and mandate reporting to the CIO.

A second key difference at SML-2 is that all work, and the person who did it, is recorded and reported. This report, along with an up-to-date list of the people available for ASM, is a major step forward. With this capability, SML-2 can introduce concepts of basic ASM management, namely that there are work requests coming in on a random basis, and using a pool of staff, these work requests must be assigned and completed in a fair and equitable manner. Higher maturity levels are needed for a formal process to assign and complete work. In SML-2, ASM management is by good ole' gut feel.

The third key difference at SML-2 is that ASM is recognized as a discipline, and with that some basic principles of the ASM discipline—namely the ASM Problem Ownership Culture and the ASM Black Box Delivery Model—come into play.

In summary, to be at SML-2 the following must be in place.

1. ASM, AD, and infrastructure must be organized into separate departments with separate managers reporting at equal levels. Each departmental manager must have the authority to implement a discipline (Methodology, Tools, certified people) correspondent to their discipline, provided it integrates with the other IT departments and aligns with the overall direction of the organization. The accountabilities and responsibilities should be clear with:

    a. Infrastructure responsible for keeping all hardware and systems software running smoothly for the organization. They are also responsible for IT security, integrity, production control, and the general safekeeping of all IT assets and documents.

    b. ASM responsible for keeping all applications running smoothly. They are mandated to reduce costs, increase reliability, and increase usability of these applications.

    c. AD responsible for all projects that require project management expertise. This includes new application development and helping infrastructure and users with new hardware and software acquisitions respectively.

2. ASM, AD, and infrastructure must retain accurate, up-to-date headcount records with people's names, addresses, phone numbers, and the workgroup (team) they are assigned to. This information is disseminated so that if there is a problem, the appropriate person to handle the problem can be contacted.

3. ASM must retain accurate ticket counts of work requests and work being done. There must be no work done without a ticket. All back-dooring (doing work for people and not recording that work) must have stopped, including internal work for other IT departments and people. Each ticket must show:

    • Identifying title which summarizes in as few words as possible the issue with the application

- A separate more detailed description of the issue and the action taken

- Date and time of occurrence

- Name of the person writing in the log who is handling the situation

4. An up-to-date inventory of applications running on the servers must be maintained. Infrastructure tracks the system software and ASM tracks the list of applications. There is no concept of application hierarchy at SML-1 or SML-2

ASM Scalability

The SML-2 best practices in ASM are scaled to reflect a small IT organization, one that is just large enough to merit having ASM as a separate department within IT, distinct and different from infrastructure. The applications environment is expected to consist of a small number of purchased packages, or a legacy in-house developed application, plus some customized development and enhancements around the packages. The packages require considerable effort to install and are somewhat complex to use and maintain. Hence, SML-2 is an informally managed ASM organization where the few non-critical applications, and the small number of people involved, can be managed inside the heads of one or two smart individuals.

ASM Organizational Capability

Organizational ASM capability at SML-2 is still non-existent. While there is the recognition that ASM exists as a discipline, the organizational capability resides in the IT manager's gut. ASM Methodology, ASM tools, and ASM certified people are not organizationally implemented.

ASM Best Practices Implemented at SML-2

SML-2 Best Practices	
1. Change Control, Security and Integrity	(1) Backup Recovery Rule (2) Data Integrity Rule (3) Testing Rule (4) Source Code Integrity Rule (5) Separate Environment Rule (6) Separation of Duties Rule (7) Window of Opportunity Rule
2. Documentation	Ticket documentation is a manually kept log of application issues: • Identifying title which summarizes in as few words as possible the issue with the application • A separate more detailed description of the issue and the action taken • Date and time of occurrence • Name of the person writing in the log who is handling the situation.
3. Problem Ownership Culture	ASM team members are members of the ASM community, who, as a discipline, take overall responsibility for all problems in all publicly used applications. On site, each ASM team member takes personal responsibility and ownership for a problem call until it is resolved. Root cause analysis is done to ensure the underlying problem is fixed, not just the symptom, so the problem never re-occurs. When the problem occurs outside of the group's immediate responsibility, initiative is taken to ensure the third party does resolve it. In smaller organizations where everyone knows everyone else personally, the problem ownership culture is more inherent. There are fewer vague "they-type" departments to put the blame on.

4. Black Box Delivery Model	Applications are separated into suites of black boxes with one and only one ASM team being responsible for changes to each black box. Formally, black box delivery model means encapsulation of Level Green Applications for purposes of ASM custodianship responsibility. In smaller IT shops, the whole ASM group may handle at most one or two application black boxes.
5. Taxonomy	n/a
6. Governance	n/a
7. Tools	n/a
8. Cyclical Life Cycle	n/a
9. Stewardship Reporting	n/a
10. Continuous Improvement Culture	n/a
11. Benchmarks and Service Levels	n/a
12. ASM Maturity Levels	n/a

SML-3 Process Utilization
ASM is a formal discipline with one automated standardized ASM process for measuring/reporting ASM size (application inventory), activity (tasks), and governance (priorities) for the whole organization.

SML-3 is real ASM. SML-3 represents ASM as the new IT discipline!

Achieving SML-3 represents outstanding achievement for any organization. It means understanding and implementing the bulk of the ASM Twelve Best Practices, which is a huge accomplishment.

SML-3 represents ASM being implemented in the organization as a discipline with ASM-specific methodology, tools, and people. It is a formally managed ASM environment following pre-defined, documented ASM-specific procedures throughout the whole corporation. Organizationally, ASM is viewed and managed as intellectual capital, with assets (application hierarchy and ASM-specific tools), procedures (ASM-specific cyclical methodology), and people (certified ASM practitioners); or, stated another way, ASM is viewed as a suite of applications managed by an Application Steering Committee utilizing IT disciplines such as ASM.

Scalability

SML-3 is industrial strength—built for large multi-application environments with mission critical applications being used by large numbers of people across multiple geographic locations. SML-3 is scalable from the largest of large to all but the smallest of IT shops. For example, in defining the application hierarchy: for smaller IT shops, a single level of abstraction can be used where Levels Blue, Green, and Yellow are all at the same level of abstraction; in extremely large, complex IT organizations, any number of levels of abstraction can be created—so long as they are presentable in a hierarchy.

Organizational Capability

At SML-3 ASM organizational capability is comprehensive, able to effectively manage even the most complex IT group using metrics of counts and activity. Counts and activity should not be underestimated. Implementing standardized Olympic-style metrics world-wide to run all ASM and motivate staff globally is no small undertaking.

ASM BEST PRACTICES IMPLEMENTED AT SML-3

SML-3 Best Practices	
1. Change Control, Security and Integrity	(1) Backup Recovery Rule
	(2) Data Integrity Rule
	(3) Testing Rule
	(4) Source Code Integrity Rule
	(5) Separate Environment Rule
	(6) Separation of Duties Rule
	(7) Window of Opportunity Rule
	(8) Change Control Process Rule
	(9) Disaster Recovery Rule

| 2. Documentation | Counts of tickets organized and reported as per the Taxonomy-ASM Best Practice #5 showing the relative priorities of tickets as per ASM Best Practice #6, using ASM-specific tools (ASM Best Practice #7). Other documents at SML-3 are the Stewardship Report (Best Practice #9), Immersion Manual, Application Support Binder, and Transition Project Charter.
The ticket documentation at SML-3 must have everything in SML-2 plus the following attributes.
• Application hierarchy in which the ticket is placed and which has the total application inventory of the organization defined in a three-level hierarchy as follows:
  o Level Blue is the top level, describing the business function at which intellectual capital (a group of application owners, users and ASM programmers) can prioritize, assign, and complete planned work on the applications such that it is aligned with the business strategy.
  o Level Green is the list of applications, named and known throughout the organization, against which problems and requests will be phoned or emailed by users. Tickets are recorded and reported at Level Green throughout the organization.
  o Level Yellow is the list of programs and purchased software that will be checked in and out of production control by ASM programmers.
• A predefined set of services—i.e. tasks—that the programmers are capable of performing. Problems, enhancements, data fixes, and information requests are examples of services. When entering a ticket, the Level Green application and the service requested must be specified.
• A predefined set of priorities that may be selected based on the importance of the service requested.
• The documented change procedure, support process and task life cycle that will be followed, according to the service requested.
• Date and time for when the ticket was received, responded to, and resolved.
To be at SML-3, these capabilities must be on-line: when a ticket is entered, a programmer must select from a list of applications and services, and in response the programmer gets the change procedure, support process, and task life cycle to be followed. |

	As well as tickets, at SML-3, the following standard documents should exist and be maintained on a regular basis: Immersion Manual: The purpose of the Immersion Manual is to align new staff to the culture of the client. The Immersion Manual answers all "first day" questions to minimize onsite training about client culture and procedures; Application Support Binder: The Application Support Binder contains all of the detailed technical and support information pertaining to a specific application or suite of applications. This documentation is to assist the ASM team in supporting the applications; and Transition Project Charter: The Transition Project Charter defines the scope of the services provided and the major task components and milestones required to ensure a successful transition of ASM from one service provider to another, or from the development team to the application support team.
3. Problem Ownership Culture	Identical to those of SML-2.
4. Black Box Delivery Model	Identical to SML-2 with additional functionality as follows: Capital differentiated from expense based on headcount assignment. The budget is headcount estimates, and the actual is headcount actuals.
5. Taxonomy	ASM requirements world-wide for the corporation are defined and shown in terms of a counted list of • Assets (application hierarchy in terms of the master taxonomy) • Activity (tickets submitted and completed on a global basis in terms of the master task taxonomy and the master procedures taxonomy) • Procedures (process to follow when an activity is performed on an asset)
6. Governance	All enhancement tickets and Level Blue Application project work are prioritized into ordinals by the Application Steering Committee. All ASM custodian teams are organized as per the team structure encoded in the ASM Tool (the corporate standard for ASM team structure).

7. Tools	The ASM Twelve Best Practices digitally codified in the ASM tool so all staff have no choice but to follow the ASM best practices to the SML as set up in the tool. The ASM Taxonomy, Life Cycle, and Methodology set up and reflected in the ASM tool. ASM people and their team assignments set up and reflected in the ASM tool.
8. Cyclical Life Cycle	Cycle #1: Identify support requirements • Define key players and system owner • Re-evaluate system • Develop maintenance strategy Cycle #2: Prepare support plan • Develop service level agreements • Identify staffing and costs • Establish Q/A and standards Cycle #3: Perform system maintenance and enhancements • Enhancements and change control • Failures, errors and support Cycle #4: Gather system measurements • Gather timesheets • Prepare statistical reports
9. Stewardship Reporting	Annual compendium of all applications organized by business function (Level Blue application) and showing assets and activity for the past year in terms of • Application inventory (all levels of abstraction) • Intellectual capital and associated costs • Application performance analysis
10. Continuous Improvement Culture	n/a
11. Benchmarks and Service Levels	n/a
12. ASM Maturity Levels	n/a

SML-4 Best Practices

ASM is a formal discipline with one automated standardized ASM process for measuring/reporting size, activity, governance; plus time, value, and cost for the whole organization.

Going from SML-3 to SML-4 means moving from an activity- and count-based approach, to a time-, value-, and cost-based approach. One might think that IT organizations are already managing based on time and value—but normally this is a budgeting and accounting view not used to drive ASM activity in the bowels of the ASM organization. At SML-4, time, value, and cost stand alongside counts and other metrics used at SML-3 to drive decision making at the programmer level.

For example, at SML-4, the activity-based approach to work continues (e.g. there are 125 tickets in the backlog) and a time- and value-based approach to work is added (e.g. there are 125 tickets in the backlog which, based on the history of tickets of that type in this application, represents 600 hours of programmer time, 330 hours of user testing time, fifty-five hours of infrastructure time…This represents a cost of $5.2 million, 25 percent of the annual carrying cost of the application of $21 million per year. Based on current intellectual capital availability, it will take one year to complete the backlog. The replacement cost of the application is $327 million).

SML-4 increases ASM management complexity and requires higher sophistication within the organization. SML-4 has numerous double-entry accounting checks and balances (e.g. time on calendars versus time on timesheets versus time on tickets; estimated time versus actual time versus benchmark standards) to validate information for accuracy. SML-4 should not be attempted until SML-3 has been in place within the total organization for several years and all staff are totally comfortable with the SML-3 processes.

Scalability

Like SML-3, SML-4 is totally scalable. From a scalability perspective, SML-4 is identical to SML-3.

Organizational Capability

Applications are assets and ASM is a discipline and metrics include time, cost and value as well as counts.

ASM BEST PRACTICES IMPLEMENTED AT SML-4

SML-4 Best Practices	
1. Change Control, Security, and Integrity	Identical to those of SML-3
2. Documentation	Tickets showing response time, resolve time, estimated time, and actual time, all compared to an industry benchmark. SML-4 requires greater sophistication and effort in that benchmarks and service levels are required for reporting. At SML-4, as well as everything at SML-3, the following additional information and documentation is required • Application importance (e.g. mission critical, critical, vital, important) and skill-set required for ASM for each Green Level application. • Benchmarks and service levels of time to respond and time to resolve based on the service requested and the application importance. These are compared to actual times to respond and to resolve, in order to report on levels of service. • Estimated time and actual time recorded on enhancement tickets. Automated time-estimate capability for quick tickets such as information requests. • Timesheets with intellectual capital capability such that time (and skill-set) recorded on timesheets can be team-linked to time recorded on tickets (and skill-set requirements) at Level Blue applications and the shrinkage (skills gap) noted.
3. Problem Ownership Culture	Identical to those of SML-3

4. Black Box Delivery Model	Same as SML-3, but capital is differentiated from expense based on FTE, timesheets, and hourly rates as opposed to just using headcount. FTE estimates and hourly rates are used for budgeting.
5. Taxonomy	ASM requirements world-wide for the corporation are defined and shown in terms of a counted list plus associated time, cost, and value of • Assets (application hierarchy in terms of the master taxonomy) • Activity (tickets submitted and completed on a global basis in terms of the master task taxonomy and the master procedures taxonomy) • Procedures (process to follow when an activity is performed on an asset) Original cost, ongoing carrying cost, and estimated replacement cost are reported for all • Assets (application hierarchy) • Procedures (task taxonomy, and procedures taxonomy)
6. Governance	All enhancement tickets and Level Blue application project work prioritized into ordinals by Application Steering committees. Knowledge by the Application Steering committee about ongoing carrying cost, and estimated replacement costs for people who are competent using the corporate ASM procedures, who are knowledgeable about the application assets and are part of the ASM team.
7. Tools	Same capability as SML-3 with the additional capability to report time, cost, and value in ASM. Also, because cost and value are within the ASM sphere, the tool must integrate seamlessly to the corporate financial reporting application.

8. Cyclical Life Cycle	Cycle #1: Identify support requirements • Define key players and system owner • Re-evaluate system • Develop maintenance strategy Cycle #2: Prepare support plan • Develop service level agreements • Identify staffing and costs • Establish Q/A and standards Cycle #3: Perform system maintenance and enhancements • Enhancements and change control • Failures, errors and support Cycle #4: Gather system measurements • Gather timesheets • Prepare statistical reports
9. Stewardship Reporting	Annual compendium of all applications organized by business function (Level Blue application) and showing assets and activity for the past year in terms of • Application inventory (all levels of abstraction) • Intellectual capital and associated costs • Application performance analysis Quarterly reporting of actual numbers versus planned numbers in the support plan for: • headcount, • costs, • application inventory, • ASM service activity • benchmarks.
10. Continuous Improvement Culture	Capability to measure and report on the results of the intrinsic desire to remove problems and fix errors so the number of issues is reduced. Continuous improvement is implemented via consistent, careful, and accurate measurement of appropriate counts and then rewarding people when they improve the reliability of an application.
11. Benchmarks and Service Levels	Activity, counts, time, and value reported against comparable industry benchmarks.

12. ASM Maturity Levels	Corporate-wide understanding of ASM maturity levels for eventual adoption/integration by other groups in the organization in preparation for movement to SML-5.

SML-5 Transparency
ASM is an integrated link in the service chain where ASM cost, value, and time are managed as sub-units of the end service or product being delivered.

SML-5 requires implementation and integration of best practices in all disciplines and functions in all the service chains in the organization. For example, CMM 4, SML-4 and ITIL (some advanced level) implemented and integrated in AD, ASM and infrastructure respectively are indicators of SML-5 capability. Furthermore SML-5 implies that the Japanese principle called kaizen can be implemented for continuous improvement of the end service. As mentioned earlier, the essence of kaizen is the notion that all disciplines in the service chain and their managers, practitioners, and workers collaborate continually to systemize the service tasks and identify incremental changes to make the end service run more smoothly. End to end statistical process control for a business function in which ASM is a small part is a sign of SML-5.

Appendix F

IT Governance Based on Government Models

Governance is government. Government is governance.

Government is based on rules. Rules are created, changed, and enforced in the general population by a subset of the population who are organized into some sort of structure and following some sort of process. Almost anything can be governed provided there is a set of rules, and a process to create and change the rules.

Here is the generic governance diagram.

GENERIC GOVERNANCE MODEL

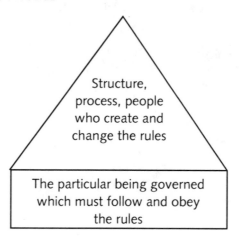

Structure, process, people who create and change the rules

The particular being governed which must follow and obey the rules

Modern government structures of most countries, states, and cities are described as having three separate branches.

1. <u>Legislative Branch</u>. Creates and changes the set of rules that all people, including the legislators, must live by. For each rule, a consequence is notated for situations where the rule is not followed.

2. <u>Executive Branch</u>. Executes and enforces the rules that the legislators have created. Watches for infractions by the general public and brings in-

dividuals it thinks have disobeyed the rules to the attention of the judicial branch.

3. <u>Judicial Branch</u>. Handles all complaints about rules not being followed, including complaints from the executive, and imposes consequences if indeed the rules were not followed.

Models of modern government are classified based on how the three branches of government are created and managed. There are four common models:

1. <u>Democracy</u>. Democracy means that the legislative, executive, and judicial branches of government are elected to office via a free vote of the people. Simple majority (of votes) is the basis for decision-making. Democracies vary, of course: sometimes the legislative branch is elected, and the judicial and executive branches are appointed by the legislators. Direct democracy means the population votes directly in a referendum to pass a rule rather than have the legislators vote on their behalf. Power emanates from the general population, who go to the polls and vote.

2. <u>Dictatorship</u>. Dictatorship means all branches of government are appointed and controlled by one person. That person comes to power and keeps power by force. The dictator's whims are the basis of decision-making. All power emanates from the dictator.

3. <u>Theocracy</u>. Theocracy means the legislators, executive, and judicial are church officials. The basis of decision-making is religious writings, which are sacrosanct and cannot be changed. Power emanates from the religion.

4. <u>Aristocracy</u>. Aristocracy means that legislators, executive, and judicial are decided by birthright and inheritance within a family. The basis of decision-making is the king. All power emanates from the king and from aristocratic families.

Infrastructure Governance (Theocracy)

If you have ever sat in a techie meeting where there is a technology discussion about which computer, which language, which database, or which software should be purchased and used, you will immediately agree with me that theocracy is the de facto governance model for infrastructure. As with religion, so it is in IT infrastructure: for any selected technology, you have both believers and nonbelievers. Irrespective of reason, believers will never convince nonbelievers and vice versa. Worse, the harder one tries to convince the other about their technology choice, the more emotionally destructive the discussion becomes.

If many technology standards (religions) are permitted in the organization, the result is total chaos. Nothing interfaces with anything else, duplicate staff must be hired to understand the different technologies, staff work in technology fiefdoms, and any integration projects are either impossible or prohibitively expensive. Religious freedom in infrastructure is not an option.

Most IT organizations, through recognition of the problems created by multi-platform, multi-technology, (multi-religion) environments have instituted theocracy-type rules whereby only certain technologies represented by certain vendors are permitted into the organization. Blocking non-standard technologies from an organization is couched in soft terms like "technology standard," but the rules are enforced with the same vigor that theocracies use to enforce religious rules. What is important is for the CIO to recognize the infrastructure governance model for what it is—a theocracy—and govern it accordingly. Religious fervor—a belief in the single selected technology—is paramount! It must be maintained in the general population at all costs.

Maintaining the "religious beliefs" with respect to the existing in-house technology standard is a challenge for the CIO. Unfortunately, technology, unlike religion, changes every few years; this means that the organizational zeal has to be moved off one standard and on to another. The task is huge and high-risk. If people are not properly converted to the new technology standard (religion), then belief in the religion and the religious leadership becomes suspect, and the theocracy faces dissension and disorder. Clearly, a change to a new technology standard should be a rare event undertaken only after careful thought and consideration. The change in standard requires a detailed plan with the rollout including several well-orchestrated presentations. The IT executive must use their oratory skills and persuasive demeanor and adopt the role of a preacher with missionary-like zeal.

Here is the infrastructure governance diagram:

INFRASTRUCTURE GOVERNANCE MODEL (THEOCRACY)

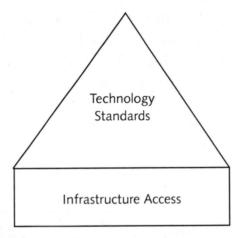

Applications Development Governance (Aristocracy)

The applications development (AD) governance model is a dictatorship. This is not my claim, but that of my predecessors in the many books and articles written about applications development.

In the classic book, The Mythical Man-Month, Frederick P. Brookes asserts that conceptual integrity is THE (his emphasis) most important consideration in AD. The "conceptual integrity in turn dictates that the design must proceed from one mind, or from a very small number of agreeing resonant minds," he says. He shows that the model works by separating the architecture effort (the aristocrats defining what happens) and setting it above the implementation effort (commoners defining how it happens).

For a metaphorical example, Brookes uses architecture. Brookes says that the architectural unity of the Cathedral of Rheims stands in glorious contrast to most European cathedrals, which are a hodge-podge of designs reflecting the fashion of the day over the many generations it took to build the cathedral. "The integrity of Rheims was achieved by the self-abnegation of eight generations of builders, each of whom sacrificed some of his ideas so that the whole might be of pure design," Brookes says.

The chief programmer teams model described in another AD classic, Chief Programmer Teams: Principles and Procedures, by Harlan Mills, is an extension and confirmation of the aristocratic governance model for AD. Mills says that good programmers are ten times more productive than bad programmers; to address this fact, Mills suggests setting up chief programmer teams where there are one programmer and nine supporting roles. This concept holds true to the aristocratic society of the past where ten specialized servants were needed to get the aristocrat through the day. It is an expensive approach, but given the inherent nature of AD, it works extremely well and is critical to success.

Hence, successful AD projects depend on implementing the vision of one or two people through an "arrogance of the aristocrats" approach to management. For success, the visionary, or leader, must have total control over all aspects of the project, and dictatorial powers to ensure the right things are done at the right time. The AD governance model, to be successful, must resemble a dictatorship—or, as Brookes says, in a more gentle reference, an aristocracy.

The problem in AD is that there are good aristocrats with correct visions of the future and bad aristocrats with wrong-headed views of the future. It is always difficult to tell which is which until the cathedral is built. Furthermore, powerful stakeholders are constantly insisting they want democratic-type input to the design, thus interfering with the underlying criteria for success: the aristocratic governance model. Mindful of the expression, "it looks like it was designed by a committee," the CIO has a difficult and challenging role in managing AD. But AD management is crucial for the success of the CIO. It is a role the CIO must play and play well. It requires total focus and attention.

Here is the applications development governance diagram:

APPLICATIONS DEVELOPMENT GOVERNANCE MODEL (ARISTOCRACY)

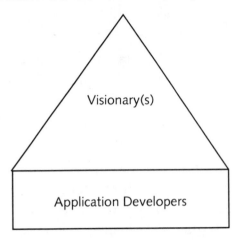

Applications Support and Maintenance Governance (Democracy)

In applications support and maintenance (ASM), the inherent governance model is totally different from that of infrastructure or AD. In ASM, there is no religion to follow, and integrity of design is not the most important consideration. The application software and its underlying technology, exemplified by that Rheims cathedral, is already built; the originator's vision is expressed and implemented. Staff in ASM just have to use, maintain, and of course, admire it. Just as the custodians of the Rheims cathedral cannot change the underlying architecture from Gothic to Romanesque, so the custodians of application software cannot change the underlying architecture from one application intent to another. Dictatorships, aristocracies, and theocracies don't work in ASM. For ASM, democracy is the best governance model.

The charm of democracy for ASM is that the model excels in bringing disparate groups with competing requirements into a process, rule-based environment where the common good prevails. Furthermore, because it is rule-based, the overhead cost and executive attention required in this model are minimal. ASM, as opposed to AD, has a flat organization run by an Application Steering Committee of "elected" representatives (application owners and stakeholders) who set priorities and provide overall direction to the custodians based on predefined rules set by the corporation. Using the U.S. model of democracy, ASM governance is described below.

ASM must start with an ASM constitution, which is the set of basic unchanging rules that all staff associated with ASM must follow. Just as new democracies often use the U.S. constitution as a starting point, new ASM organizations should use the ASM Twelve Best Practices described in this book as a starting point.

The ASM constitution is not meant to be the complete set of rules describing the whole ASM process in the whole organization. It is an overview with which all ASM procedures created and followed within the organization must align. Within the organization, there will be a large variety of processes to follow for different applications, depending on criticality, importance of request, geographic location, and user discipline. The set of all rules for all ASM is huge and is called the ASM methodology. In our American government analogy, as well as the U.S. constitution, there are thousands of other rules that are enacted depending on the geographic area (Alaska versus Delaware), different situations (rules for driving, rules for corporations, rules for private property) that are not part of the U.S. constitution. For a starting point, new ASM shops should use an existing ASM methodology. The ASM methodology selected can and will change from site to site and location to location depending on local requirements. However, the ASM constitution (the Twelve Best Practices) should always override and apply to all sites, all locations, and all situations.

The power of the democratic model of governance is that once the rules are set up, it just runs. Power changes hands, people come and go, rules get changed; all without the need of a CxO executive getting involved. Granted, the challenge of setting up an ASM democratic governance model is not small. Rules have to be created, and people have to accept, learn, and participate in the model. But the results are well worth the initial effort.

The ASM governance model, showing the U.S. government equivalent in italics, is described below. Note that there is a separate Application Steering

Committee for each Level Blue application in the corporation.

Application Steering Committee - Legislative

- Adopts the ASM Twelve Best Practices (U.S. constitution).

- Has ultimate authority on all aspects of ASM governance for the Level Blue Applications (a vote in Congress dictates ultimate decision).

- Sets and approves the overall budget for ASM custodianship of each Level Blue Application (congressional budget).

- Is a focal point for their corporate department's needs and requirements with respect to the application (represents their constituents in Washington).

- Discusses and agrees on priorities of application work requests (votes on bills before Congress).

- Approves any ASM taxonomy (and other appropriate parts of the ASM methodology) additions and changes (enacts new laws).

Application Custodian - Executive

- Follows and obeys the ASM Twelve Best Practices and the locally enacted ASM methodology (U.S. president's oath of office).

- Completes work assignments based on the application work priorities set by the Application Steering Committee. The ASM discipline resides here. (U.S. government bureaucracy.)

- Stays within the budget (U.S. president has to ask Congress for more money).

- Publishes and disseminates rules and rule changes enacted by the Application Steering Committee to its staff.

Auditors - Judicial

- Oversees the ASM methodology to ensure it is compliant with the ASM Twelve Best Practices and other external practices such as Sarbanes Oxley (U.S. Supreme Court constitutional rulings).

- Handles complaints about non-compliance. Generates "rulings" on whether or not certain situations are or are not compliant (handles court cases).

- Initiates audits to ensure the ASM Twelve Best Practices and the ASM methodology is being adhered to (public inquiries).

Another charm of rule-based democracies is that they are conducive to contractual arrangements between entities. Unlike dictatorships (AD) where rule interpretation is based on the current whim of the dictator, in democracies there is a culture of understanding and following rules. This means that contracts for ASM services are relatively easy for all parties to create, understand, and follow, whereas contracts for AD services or infrastructure services are inherently problematic. In AD and infrastructure, the governance must be inherently autocratic because the future is so unpredictable. Hence, outsourcing ASM is contractually straightforward, whereas outsourcing AD or infrastructure is contractually very difficult.

Each ASM Contract will be unique but have common clauses as follows. Again, for clarity, American government equivalent terminology is shown in bracketed italics.

1. **Term** (begin date and end date). There is an ability to end the term prematurely but only via extensive due process detailed in the termination clause (impeachment process). The process for renewal (election process) is also detailed, but there is no obligation to renew.

2. **Custodianship Services Required.** The application hierarchy (inventory of government assets) and the list of services to be provided (List of services the government is expected to provide for the people—foreign affairs, roads, and infrastructure, etc.) must be a part of the contract.

a.   The contract is for application custodianship only. The application ownership remains with the client. (The USA is owned by the American people, not by the American government)

b.   The scope of custodianship responsibilities—application inventory and list of services—can be increased or decreased during the term if both parties agree. However, the scoped services cannot be moved to another service provider during the term unless the contract is first terminated. (The American people cannot switch from a Republican president to a Democratic contender in midterm).

c.   A change in scope of custodianship responsibilities does not automatically imply a change in headcount or costs. Which headcount is providing services (budget) is decided solely by the Application Steering Committee. Work is prioritized and done within this headcount. (Congress and the elected president tell bureaucrats how much they can spend, not vica versa. Bureaucrats do the best they can within the funding provided. Governments constantly face unlimited demand for services with limited ability to afford them. They must prioritize).

d.   All work priorities and work direction comes from the Application Steering Committee, not from individual application users. (Bureaucrats report to Congress, who in turn are responsible to the American people. The U.S. is too big for direct democracy to work).

e.   Next year's planned headcount (U.S. budget) is decided by due process. Actual headcount can vary, increase or decrease, from the plan only if due process is followed. (Congress must vote on budget changes).

3.   **Costs**. Price per headcount. Price per headcount with actual headcount provides invoices (budget expenditures). Price per headcount, and/or pricing formulas, cannot be changed unless both parties agree.

4.   **Service Levels**. Commitments (election promises) made by service pro-

viders (Democrats or Republicans) as a condition for being selected as application custodian.

An ASM contract should exist, irrespective of whether the sourcing strategy is in-house or outsourced. It should be a stable document, almost like a constitution, that lasts through changes in application custodians, application owners, and Application Steering Committees. It should describe intent as well as rules and be something that is learned and understood by all.

A note of caution with respect to ASM contracts and the service levels agreements entrenched in many current outsourcing contracts: ASM, like all democratic institutions, faces an infinite demand for services from its constituents that could never possibly be satisfied. Furthermore, unforeseen changes in the business climate (e.g. war in government) can require instantaneous changes in priorities for services. Writing legally binding contracts containing predefined services and service levels for seven-year intervals is extremely risky. Instead, ASM benchmarks supported by strong ASM methodology and ASM tools should be inherent in the service and culture of the service provider. The ASM contract, as described above, can then focus on governance, termination, and unit-pricing clauses.

Here is the ASM governance diagram:

ASM GOVERNANCE MODEL (DEMOCRACY)

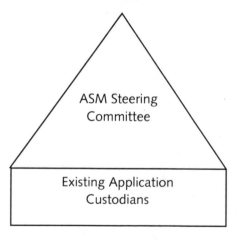

ASM Steering
Committee

Existing Application
Custodians

Once the ASM governance is properly set up in the organization with the structure, process and rules, it really does run on "auto-pilot." There is minimal effort required from either the CIO or IT executives because the application owners and stakeholders run it. Hence, once good ASM Governance is established, the CIO can and should focus on AD.

Appendix G

ASM Maturity Level Assessment – Sample Queries

Activity/Ticket Repository - ASM Maturity Criteria
Taxonomy Set-up 　1. Application Taxonomy identified　(Application Portfolio: Application Hierarchy, Application Importance, Skill-set). 　2. Task Taxonomy identified　　(Task Type, Task Lifecycle, Task Priority, Task Value, Task Occurrence). 　3. Procedures Taxonomy identified　(Change Procedure and Support Process). 　4. Ticket Taxonomy identified　　(ASM Service Template and ASM Service Benchmark). 　5. ASM-specific tool used for all of the above.
Tickets Recorded and Managed 　1. All requests are recorded as tickets and do not allow "backdooring". 　2. Actual/estimated, start/end dates are updated on maintenance and enhancement tickets (not support). 　3. ASM service status updated appropriately. 　4. ASM-specific tool used for all of the above.
Team Status Report 　1. Verify that the ASM service status is updated and current. 　2. Ensure that at least all of the Top 10 items have estimates (not support tickets). 　3. Ensure that all effort, remaining, actual, and estimate dates are updated. 　4. ASM-specific tool used for all of the above.
Top 10 Report Used 　1. Ensure there is one report for each steering committee. 　2. ASM-specific tool used for Top 10 Report.
Resolved Ticket Report Used 　1. Ensure that tickets, other than support tickets, have at least a minimum effort applied. 　2. ASM-specific tool used for resolved ticket report.
Unresolved Ticket Report Used 　1. Ensure that appropriate tickets are closed. 　2. ASM-specific tool used for unresolved tickets report.

Steering Committee Reports
1. The Top 10 Report: review all priority Items and adjust priorities at Steering Committee's request.
2. The Unresolved Report: discuss status of new and backlogged tickets.
3. The Unresolved Report: review any items not on the Top 10 and see if they need to move there now.
4. The Resolved Report: discuss tickets that were resolved since the last meeting.
5. ASM-specific tool used for all of the above.

Received Tickets Report
1. Discuss new tickets received from last report.
2. ASM-specific tool used for received tickets report.

Stewardship Report
1. Create an annual Stewardship report.
2. Create and present Stewardship report presentation.
3. ASM-specific tool used in the creation of this report.

Assignment/Timesheet Repository - ASM Maturity Criteria

Current Time Sheets
1. Automated timesheet is used to produce accurate timekeeping/management reporting.

My/My Staff Reporting
1. Vacation/sick/lieu time reports are used.

Site Administration
1. Affiliations are understood.
2. Assignment roles are understood.
3. Staff associations are understood.
4. Workgroup Template is understood.
5. Workgroups are understood.
6. Timecode categories and series are understood.
7. Calendars and submission periods are understood.

Data Administration
1. Ensure all staffing changes are updated (check corporate headcount report or workgroups/assignments).
2. Process to approve employees timesheets is used.

Corporate-Wide Reporting Used
1. Business structure handbook is utilized.
2. Headcount reports are utilized.
3. Turnover staff reports are utilized.
4. Staff utilization reports are utilized.
5. Time sheet reports are utilized.
6. ASM-specific tool is used for all of the above.

Lines of Business Defined
1. Lines of business are defined per the Taxonomy
2. A Line of Business is clearly associated with a single team within your group (support of application—level blue).
3. Reports are run based on the line of business.
4. ASM-specific tool is used to define Lines of Business.

Training/Certification Repository - ASM Maturity Criteria

Public
1. External manuals: Oracle, PowerBuilder, IBM OS/390 or other manuals.
2. Internal documents: speeches, whitepapers, or presentations.
3. Technical conference material.
4. Past issues of the company newsletter.
5. Employee benefits.
6. Travel expense.

Employees
1. ASM certification.
2. ASM methodology book.
3. ASM forms/templates.
4. Education.
5. Lunch and Learn Material on Twelve Best Practices.

Administration
1. Human resources.

Governance Repository - ASM Maturity Criteria

Site Specific Data Stored
1. Store Steering Committee Meeting Agenda and Minutes.
2. Store Team Status Meeting Agenda and Minutes.
3. Store Other Site Specific Data.

ASM Methodology - ASM Maturity Criteria

ASM Methodology Book
1. All employees have access to the internet or have a hard copy of ASM Methodology Book.
2. All employees are aware of how to locate a copy of ASM Methodology Book.
3. All of your ASM teams follow the ASM Methodology.
4. ASM forms and templates are used as needed.

Team Status Meeting
1. There are team status Meetings.
2. Verify the team is prioritizing work not on Top 10.
3. Verify that priority items are being worked on.
4. Minutes of the meeting are stored until the next report.

Steering Committee Meeting
1. There are Steering Committee Meetings.
2. Key business and IT members sit on the Steering Committees.
3. Steering Committee meets regularly.
4. Steering Committee sets the work priorities.
5. Resource availability is considered when determining start and end dates.
6. Minutes of the meeting are distributed and stored.

Immersion Manual
1. An immersion manual has been created.
2. It is updated appropriately.
3. Team members are informed of the immersion manual.
4. It follows the ASM Methodology Format.

Application Support Binder
1. An Application Support Binder has been created for each application.
2. It is updated appropriately.
3. Team members are informed of the support binder.
4. It follows the ASM Methodology Format.

Appendix H

IT / Business Alignment Process

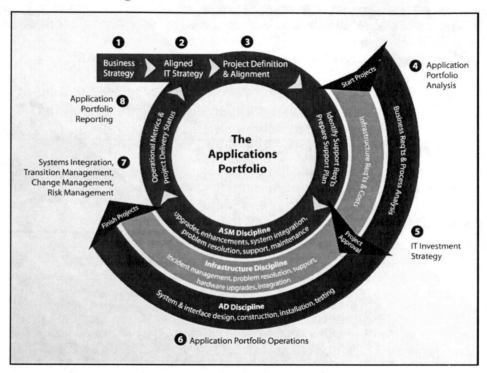

❶ Business Strategy

The Corporate Business Strategy drives the IT Strategy, Objectives, Investment Decisions and Execution Plans to provide an information environment to effectively support the company's decision making and regulatory requirements.

❷ Aligned IT Strategy

The Business and IT Strategy are aligned on an ongoing continuous improvement basis as more performance feedback is received following the execution and reporting of results. This alignment provides the information environment with the agility to respond to changing business environments and the resultant changes in corporate Business Strategy. The overall 'control management' is defined consistent with the SOX guiding principles and objectives.

❸ Project Definition and Alignment

This component identifies new opportunities – both from a technology viewpoint and a business viewpoint – which could potentially help IT and the business meet its strategic objectives.

❹ Application Portfolio Analysis

This component defines the existing computer applications in the company plus the new IT projects that could potentially be approved to support the Business Strategy to achieve the performance targets. Both existing computer applications and new projects are defined in terms of the 3 IT disciplines: Applications Support and Maintenance (ASM), Infrastructure (IFS), and Applications Development (AD).   They are also both evaluated and defined to align with the corporate business systems architecture which defines the information environment desired to meet the long term decision making and regulatory needs of the company.

❺ IT Investment Strategy

The IT Investment Strategy defines the guiding principles and decision criteria for approval of the systems development projects and enhancement opportunities identified in the prior phase. By design, the opportunities in the portfolio exceed the funding or budget capability to ensure there is a continuous high-grading of business opportunities for approval and execution.

❻ Application Portfolio Operations

Once the Investment Strategy and all its component projects are approved, IT moves into the execution phase where the business requirements are defined in more detail and the business processes are evaluated for business improvement opportunities. Opportunities are continuously sought to improve the business controls as part of the business process improvement.

➐ Systems Integration, Transition Management, Change Management, Risk Management

Moving projects from the good idea phase into the mainstream of the business without impacting normal day to day operations is what this phase is all about.

➑ Application Portfolio Reporting

This loop back into the business planning process aligns IT with the normal business reporting cycle: plan versus actual on a quarterly basis.

Appendix I

Example Frameworks for Standardized Procedures

Examples of Best Practice Frameworks, Associations, Disciplines

Best Pracitce	Initial Origins	A Website Reference (valid at time of printing)
CMMI	Process Maturity & Application Development	www.sei.cmu.edu/cmmi/
COBIT	IT Audit	www.isaca.org
ISO	Manufacturing / Specifications	www.iso.org
ITIL	IT Infrastructure	www.itil.co.uk
MOF	Microsoft / ITIL	www.microsoft.com/technet/itsolutions/cits/mo/mof/
Six Sigma	Manufacturing/ Deming Quality	www.isssp.com
SMART	IT Applications Support and Maintenance	www.RISGlobal.com www.SupportApps.com
SOX	Government Regulation	www.aicpa.org
HDI	Help Desk	www.thinkhdi.com
AGILE	Software Development	www.agilemanifesto.org

AFTERWORD

"IT Doesn't Matter" by Nicholas G. Carr & "Does IT Matter? An HBR Debate"

Harvard Business Review, reprinted by permission

"IT Doesn't Matter" by Nicholas G. Carr

Nicholas G. Carr *is HBR's editor-at-large. He edited The Digital Enterprise, a collection of HBR articles published by Harvard Business School Press in 2001, and has written for the Financial Times, Business 2.0, and the Industry Standard in addition to HBR.*

In 1968, a young Intel engineer named Ted Hoff found a way to put the circuits necessary for computer processing onto a tiny piece of silicon. His invention of the microprocessor spurred a series of technological breakthroughs – desktop computers, local and wide area networks, enterprise software, and the Internet – that have transformed the business world. Today, no one would dispute that information technology has become the backbone of commerce. It underpins the operations of individual companies, ties together far-flung supply chains, and, increasingly, links businesses to the customers they serve. Hardly a dollar or a euro changes hands anymore without the aid of computer systems.

As IT's power and presence have expanded, companies have come to view it as a resource ever more critical to their success, a fact clearly reflected in their spending habits. In 1965, according to a study by the U.S. Department of Commerce's Bureau of Economic Analysis, less than 5% of the capital expenditures of American companies went to information technology. After the introduction of the personal computer in the early 1980s, that percentage rose to 15%. By the early 1990s, it had reached more than 30%, and by the end of the decade it had hit nearly 50%. Even with the recent sluggishness in technology spending, businesses around the world continue to spend well over $2 trillion a year on IT.

But the veneration of IT goes much deeper than dollars. It is evident as well in the shifting attitudes of top managers. Twenty years ago, most executives looked down on computers as proletarian tools – glorified typewriters and calculators – best relegated to low level employees like secretaries, analysts, and technicians. It was the rare executive who would let his fingers touch a keyboard, much less incorporate information technology into his strategic thinking. Today, that has changed completely. Chief executives now routinely talk about the strategic value of information technology, about how they can use IT to gain a competitive edge, about the "digitization" of their business models. Most have appointed chief information officers to their senior management teams, and many have hired strategy consulting firms to provide fresh ideas on how to leverage their IT investments for differentiation and advantage.

Behind the change in thinking lies a simple assumption: that as IT's potency and ubiquity have increased, so too has its strategic value. It's a reasonable assumption, even an intuitive one. But it's mistaken. What makes a resource truly strategic – what gives it the capacity to be the basis for a sustained competitive advantage – is not ubiquity but scarcity. You only gain an edge over rivals by having or doing something that they can't have or do. By now, the core functions of IT – data storage, data processing, and data transport – have become available and affordable to all.[1] Their very power and presence have begun to transform them from potentially strategic resources into commodity factors of production. They are becoming costs of doing business that must be paid by all but provide distinction to none.

IT is best seen as the latest in a series of broadly adopted technologies that have reshaped industry over the past two centuries – from the steam engine and the railroad to the telegraph and the telephone to the electric generator and the internal combustion engine. For a brief period, as they were being built into the infrastructure of commerce, all these technologies opened opportunities for forward-looking companies to gain real advantages. But as their availability increased and their cost decreased – as they became ubiquitous – they became commodity inputs. From a strategic standpoint, they became invisible; they no longer mattered. That is exactly what is happening to information technology today, and the implications for corporate IT management are profound.

Vanishing Advantage

Many commentators have drawn parallels between the expansion of IT, particularly the Internet, and the rollouts of earlier technologies. Most of the comparisons, though, have

---

1. "Information technology" is a fuzzy term. In this article, it is used in its common current sense, as denoting the technologies used for processing, storing, and transporting information in digital form.

focused on either the investment pattern associated with the technologies – the boom-to-bust cycle – or the technologies' roles in reshaping the operations of entire industries or even economies. Little has been said about the way the technologies influence, or fail to influence, competition at the firm level. Yet it is here that history offers some of its most important lessons to managers.

A distinction needs to be made between proprietary technologies and what might be called infrastructural technologies. Proprietary technologies can be owned, actually or effectively, by a single company. A pharmaceutical firm, for example, may hold a patent on a particular compound that serves as the basis for a family of drugs. An industrial manufacturer may discover an innovative way to employ a process technology that competitors find hard to replicate. A company that produces consumer goods may acquire exclusive rights to a new packaging material that gives its product a longer shelf life than competing brands. As long as they remain protected, proprietary technologies can be the foundations for long-term strategic advantages, enabling companies to reap higher profits than their rivals.

Infrastructural technologies, in contrast, offer far more value when shared than when used in isolation. Imagine yourself in the early nineteenth century, and suppose that one manufacturing company held the rights to all the technology required to create a railroad. If it wanted to, that company could just build proprietary lines between its suppliers, its factories, and its distributors and run its own locomotives and railcars on the tracks. And it might well operate more efficiently as a result. But, for the broader economy, the value produced by such an arrangement would be trivial compared with the value that would be produced by building an open rail network connecting many companies and many buyers. The characteristics and economics of infrastructural technologies, whether railroads or telegraph lines or power generators, make it inevitable that they will be broadly shared – that they will become part of the general business infrastructure.

In the earliest phases of its buildout, however, an infrastructural technology can take the form of a proprietary technology. As long as access to the technology is restricted – through physical limitations, intellectual property rights, high costs, or a lack of standards – a company can use it to gain advantages over rivals. Consider the period between the construction of the first electric power stations, around 1880, and the wiring of the electric grid early in the twentieth century. Electricity remained a scarce resource during this time, and those manufacturers able to tap into it – by, for example, building their plants near generating stations – often gained an important edge. It was no coincidence that the largest U.S. manufacturer of nuts and bolts at the turn of the century, Plumb, Burdict, and Barnard, located its factory near Niagara Falls in New York, the site of one of the earliest large-scale hydroelectric power plants.

Companies can also steal a march on their competitors by having superior insight into the use of a new technology. The introduction of electric power again provides a good example. Until the end of the nineteenth century, most manufacturers relied on water pressure or steam to operate their machinery. Power in those days came from a single, fixed source – a waterwheel at the side of a mill, for instance – and required an elaborate system of pulleys and gears to distribute it to individual workstations throughout the plant. When electric generators first became available, many manufacturers simply adopted them as a replacement single-point source, using them to power the existing system of pulleys and gears. Smart manufacturers, however, saw that one of the great advantages of electric power is that it is easily distributable – that it can be brought directly to workstations. By wiring their plants and installing electric motors in their machines, they were able to dispense with the cumbersome, inflexible, and costly gearing systems, gaining an important efficiency advantage over their slower-moving competitors.

In addition to enabling new, more efficient operating methods, infrastructural technologies often lead to broader market changes. Here, too, a company that sees what's coming can gain a step on myopic rivals. In the mid-1800s, when America started to lay down rail lines in earnest, it was already possible to transport goods over long distances – hundreds of steamships plied the country's rivers. Businessmen probably assumed that rail transport would essentially follow the steamship model, with some incremental enhancements. In fact, the greater speed, capacity, and reach of the railroads fundamentally changed the structure of American industry. It suddenly became economical to ship finished products, rather than just raw materials and industrial components, over great distances, and the mass consumer market came into being. Companies that were quick to recognize the broader opportunity rushed to build large-scale, mass-production factories. The resulting economies of scale allowed them to crush the small, local plants that until then had dominated manufacturing.

The trap that executives often fall into, however, is assuming that opportunities for advantage will be available indefinitely. In actuality, the window for gaining advantage from an infrastructural technology is open only briefly. When the technology's commercial potential begins to be broadly appreciated, huge amounts of cash are inevitably invested in it, and its buildout proceeds with extreme speed. Railroad tracks, telegraph wires, power lines – all were laid or strung in a frenzy of activity (a frenzy so intense in the case of rail lines that it cost hundreds of laborers their lives). In the 30 years between 1846 and 1876, reports Eric Hobsbawm in *The Age of Capital*, the world's total rail trackage increased from 17,424 kilometers to 309,641 kilometers. During this same period, total steamship tonnage also exploded, from 139,973 to 3,293,072 tons. The telegraph system spread even more swiftly. In Continental Europe, there were just 2,000 miles of telegraph wires in 1849; 20 years later, there were 110,000. The pattern continued with electrical power. The number of central stations operated by utilities grew from 468 in 1889 to 4,364 in 1917, and the average capacity of each increased more than tenfold. (For a discussion of the dangers of overinvestment, see the sidebar [at the end of the article] "Too Much of a Good Thing.")

By the end of the buildout phase, the opportunities for individual advantage are largely gone. The rush to invest leads to more competition, greater capacity, and falling prices, making the technology broadly accessible and affordable. At the same time, the buildout forces users to adopt universal technical standards, rendering proprietary systems obsolete. Even the way the technology is used begins to become standardized, as best practices come to be widely understood and emulated. Often, in fact, the best practices end up being built into the infrastructure itself; after electrification, for example, all new factories were constructed with many well-distributed power outlets. Both the technology and its modes of use become, in effect, commoditized. The only meaningful advantage most companies can hope to gain from an infrastructural technology after its buildout is a cost advantage – and even that tends to be very hard to sustain.

That's not to say that infrastructural technologies don't continue to influence competition. They do, but their influence is felt at the macroeconomic level, not at the level of the individual company. If a particular country, for instance, lags in installing the technology – whether it's a national rail network, a power grid, or a communication infrastructure – its domestic industries will suffer heavily. Similarly, if an industry lags in harnessing the power of the technology, it will be vulnerable to displacement. As always, a company's fate is tied to broader forces affecting its region and its industry. The point is, however, that the technology's potential for differentiating one company from the pack – its strategic potential – inexorably declines as it becomes accessible and affordable to all.

The Commoditization of IT

Although more complex and malleable than its predecessors, IT has all the hallmarks of an infrastructural technology. In fact, its mix of characteristics guarantees particularly rapid commoditization. IT is, first of all, a transport mechanism – it carries digital information just as railroads carry goods and power grids carry electricity. And like any transport mechanism, it is far more valuable when shared than when used in isolation. The history of IT in business has been a history of increased interconnectivity and interoperability, from mainframe time-sharing to minicomputer-based local area networks to broader Ethernet networks and on to the Internet. Each stage in that progression has involved greater standardization of the technology and, at least recently, greater homogenization of its functionality. For most business applications today, the benefits of customization would be overwhelmed by the costs of isolation.

IT is also highly replicable. Indeed, it is hard to imagine a more perfect commodity than a byte of data – endlessly and perfectly reproducible at virtually no cost. The near-infinite scalability of many IT functions, when combined with technical standardization, dooms most proprietary applications to economic obsolescence. Why write your own application for word processing or e-mail or, for that matter, supply-chain management when you can buy a ready-made, state-of-the-art application for a fraction of the cost? But it's not just the software that is replicable. Because most business activities and processes have come to be embedded in software, they become replicable, too. When companies buy a generic application, they buy a generic process as well. Both the cost savings and the interoperability benefits make the sacrifice of distinctiveness unavoidable.

The arrival of the Internet has accelerated the commoditization of IT by providing a perfect delivery channel for generic applications. More and more, companies will fulfill their IT requirements simply by purchasing fee-based "Web services" from third parties – similar to the way they currently buy electric power or telecommunications services. Most of the major business-technology vendors, from Microsoft to IBM, are trying to position themselves as IT utilities, companies that will control the provision of a diverse range of business applications over what is now called, tellingly, "the grid." Again, the upshot is ever greater homogenization of IT capabilities, as more companies replace customized applications with generic ones. (For more on the challenges facing IT companies, see the sidebar [at the end of the article] "What About the Vendors?")

Finally, and for all the reasons already discussed, IT is subject to rapid price deflation. When Gordon Moore made his famously prescient assertion that the density of circuits on a computer chip would double every two years, he was making a prediction about the coming explosion in processing power. But he was also making a prediction about the coming free fall in the price of computer functionality. The cost of processing power has dropped relentlessly, from $480 per million instructions per second (MIPS) in 1978 to $50 per MIPS in 1985 to $4 per MIPS in 1995, a trend that continues unabated. Similar declines have occurred in the cost of data storage and transmission. The rapidly increasing affordability of IT functionality has not only democratized the computer revolution, it has destroyed one of the most important potential barriers to competitors. Even the most cutting-edge IT capabilities quickly become available to all.

It's no surprise, given these characteristics, that IT's evolution has closely mirrored that of earlier infrastructural technologies. Its buildout has been every bit as breathtaking as that of the railroads (albeit with considerably fewer fatalities). Consider some statistics. During the last quarter of the twentieth century, the computational power of a microprocessor increased by a factor of 66,000. In the dozen years from 1989 to 2001, the number of host computers connected to the Internet grew from 80,000 to more than 125 million. Over the last ten years, the number of sites on the World Wide Web has grown from zero to nearly 40 million. And since the 1980s, more than 280 million miles of fiber-optic cable have been installed – enough, as *Business Week* recently noted, to "circle the earth 11,320 times." (See the sidebar [at the end of the article] "The Sprint to Commoditization.")

As with earlier infrastructural technologies, IT provided forward-looking companies many opportunities for competitive advantage early in its buildout, when it could still be "owned" like a proprietary technology. A classic example is American Hospital Supply. A leading distributor of medical supplies, AHS introduced in 1976 an innovative system called Analytic Systems Automated Purchasing, or ASAP, that enabled hospitals to order goods electronically. Developed in-house, the innovative system used proprietary software running on a mainframe computer, and hospital purchasing agents accessed it through terminals at their sites. Because more efficient ordering enabled hospitals to reduce their inventories – and thus their costs – customers were quick to embrace the system. And because it was proprietary to AHS, it effectively locked out competitors. For several years, in fact, AHS was the only distributor offering electronic ordering, a competitive advantage that led to years of superior financial results. From 1978 to 1983, AHS's sales and profits rose at annual rates of 13% and 18%, respectively – well above industry averages.

AHS gained a true competitive advantage by capitalizing on characteristics of infrastructural technologies that are common in the early stages of their buildouts, in particular their high cost and lack of standardization. Within a decade, however, those barriers to competition were crumbling. The arrival of personal computers and packaged software, together with the emergence of networking standards, was rendering proprietary communication systems unattractive to their users and uneconomical to their owners. Indeed, in an ironic, if predictable, twist, the closed nature and outdated technology of AHS's system turned it from an asset to a liability. By the dawn of the 1990s, after AHS had merged with Baxter Travenol to form Baxter International, the company's senior executives had come to view ASAP as "a millstone around their necks," according to a Harvard Business School case study.

Myriad other companies have gained important advantages through the innovative deployment of IT. Some, like American Airlines with its Sabre reservation system, Federal Express with its package-tracking system, and Mobil Oil with its automated Speedpass payment system, used IT to gain particular operating or marketing advantages – to leapfrog the competition in one process or activity. Others, like Reuters with its 1970s financial information network or, more recently, eBay with its Internet auctions, had superior insight into the way IT would fundamentally change an industry and were able to stake out commanding positions. In a few cases, the dominance companies gained through IT innovation conferred additional advantages, such as scale economies and brand recognition, that have proved more durable than the original technological edge. Wal-Mart and Dell Computer are renowned examples of firms that have been able to turn temporary technological advantages into enduring positioning advantages.

But the opportunities for gaining IT-based advantages are already dwindling. Best practices are now quickly built into software or otherwise replicated. And as for IT-spurred industry transformations, most of the ones that are going to happen have likely already happened or are in the process of happening. Industries and markets will continue to evolve, of course, and some will undergo fundamental changes – the future of the music business, for example, continues to be in doubt. But history shows that the power of an infrastructural technology to transform industries always diminishes as its buildout nears completion.

While no one can say precisely when the buildout of an infrastructural technology has concluded, there are many signs that the IT buildout is much closer to its end than its beginning. First, IT's power is outstripping most of the business needs it fulfills. Second, the price of essential IT functionality has dropped to the point where it is more or less affordable to all. Third, the capacity of the universal distribution network (the Internet) has caught up with demand – indeed, we already have considerably more fiber-optic capacity than we need. Fourth, IT vendors are rushing to position themselves as commodity suppliers or even as utilities. Finally, and most definitively, the investment bubble has burst, which historically has been a clear indication that an infrastructural technology is reaching the end of its buildout. A few companies may still be able to wrest advantages from highly specialized applications that don't offer strong economic incentives for replication, but those firms will be the exceptions that prove the rule.

At the close of the 1990s, when Internet hype was at full boil, technologists offered grand visions of an emerging "digital future." It may well be that, in terms of business strategy at least, the future has already arrived.

From Offense to Defense

So what should companies do? From a practical standpoint, the most important lesson to be learned from earlier infrastructural technologies may be this: When a resource becomes essential to competition but inconsequential to strategy, the risks it creates become more important than the advantages it provides. Think of electricity. Today, no company builds its business strategy around its electricity usage, but even a brief lapse in supply can be devastating (as some California businesses discovered during the energy crisis of 2000). The operational risks associated with IT are many – technical glitches, obsolescence, service outages, unreliable vendors or partners, security breaches, even terrorism – and some have become magnified as companies have moved from tightly controlled, proprietary systems to open, shared ones. Today, an IT disruption can paralyze a company's ability to make its products, deliver its services, and connect with its customers, not to mention foul its reputation. Yet few companies have done a thorough job of identifying and tempering their vulnerabilities. Worrying about what might go wrong may not be as glamorous a job as speculating about the future, but it is a more essential job right now. (See the sidebar [at the end of the article] "New Rules for IT Management.")

In the long run, though, the greatest IT risk facing most companies is more prosaic than a catastrophe. It is, simply, overspending. IT may be a commodity, and its costs may fall rapidly enough to ensure that any new capabilities are quickly shared, but the very fact that it is entwined with so many business functions means that it will continue to consume a large portion of corporate spending. For most companies, just staying in business will require big outlays for IT. What's important – and this holds true for any commodity input – is to be able to separate essential investments from ones that are discretionary, unnecessary, or even counterproductive.

At a high level, stronger cost management requires more rigor in evaluating expected returns from systems investments, more creativity in exploring simpler and cheaper alternatives, and a greater openness to outsourcing and other partnerships. But most companies can also reap significant savings by simply cutting out waste. Personal computers are a good example. Every year, businesses purchase more than 100 million PCs, most of which replace older models. Yet the vast majority of workers who use PCs rely on only a few simple applications – word processing, spreadsheets, e-mail, and Web browsing. These applications have been technologically mature for years; they require only a fraction of the computing power provided by today's microprocessors. Nevertheless, companies continue to roll out across-the-board hardware and software upgrades.

Much of that spending, if truth be told, is driven by vendors' strategies. Big hardware and software suppliers have become very good at parceling out new features and capabilities in ways that force companies into buying new computers, applications, and networking equipment much more frequently than they need to. The time has come for IT buyers to throw their weight around, to negotiate contracts that ensure the long-term usefulness of their PC investments and impose hard limits on upgrade costs. And if vendors balk, companies should be willing to explore cheaper solutions, including open-source applications and bare-bones network PCs, even if it means sacrificing features. If a company needs evidence of the kind of money that might be saved, it need only look at Microsoft's profit margin.

In addition to being passive in their purchasing, companies have been sloppy in their use of IT. That's particularly true with data storage, which has come to account for more than half of many companies' IT expenditures. The bulk of what's being stored on corporate networks has little to do with making products or serving customers – it consists of employees' saved e-mails and files, including terabytes of spam, MP3s, and video clips. *Computerworld* estimates that as much as 70% of the storage capacity of a typical Windows network is wasted – an enormous unnecessary expense. Restricting employees' ability to save files indiscriminately and indefinitely may seem distasteful to many managers, but it can have a real impact on the bottom line. Now that IT has become the dominant capital expense for most businesses, there's no excuse for waste and sloppiness.

Given the rapid pace of technology's advance, delaying IT investments can be another powerful way to cut costs – while also reducing a firm's chance of being saddled with buggy or soon-to-be-obsolete technology. Many companies, particularly during the 1990s, rushed their IT investments either because they hoped to capture a first-mover advantage or because they feared being left behind. Except in very rare cases, both the hope and the fear were unwarranted. The smartest users of technology – here again, Dell and Wal-Mart stand out – stay well back from the cutting edge, waiting to make purchases until standards and best practices solidify. They let their impatient competitors shoulder the high costs of experimentation, and then they sweep past them, spending less and getting more.

Some managers may worry that being stingy with IT dollars will damage their competitive positions. But studies of corporate IT spending consistently show that greater expenditures rarely translate into superior financial results. In fact, the opposite is usually true. In 2002, the consulting firm Alinean compared the IT expenditures and the financial results of 7,500 large U.S. companies and discovered that the top performers tended to be among the most tightfisted. The 25 companies that delivered the highest economic returns, for example, spent on average just 0.8% of their revenues on IT, while the typical company spent 3.7%. A recent study by Forrester Research showed, similarly, that the most lavish spenders on IT rarely post the best results. Even Oracle's Larry Ellison, one of the great technology salesmen, admitted in a recent interview that "most companies spend too much [on IT] and get very little in return." As the opportunities for IT-based advantage continue to narrow, the penalties for overspending will only grow.

IT management should, frankly, become boring. The key to success, for the vast majority of companies, is no longer to seek advantage aggressively but to manage costs and risks meticulously. If, like many executives, you've begun to take a more defensive posture toward IT in the last two years, spending more frugally and thinking more pragmatically, you're already on the right course. The challenge will be to maintain that discipline when the business cycle strengthens and the chorus of hype about IT's strategic value rises anew.

SIDEBARS

Too Much of a Good Thing

As many experts have pointed out, the overinvestment in information technology in the 1990s echoes the overinvestment in railroads in the 1860s. In both cases, companies and individuals, dazzled by the seemingly unlimited commercial possibilities of the technologies, threw large quantities of money away on half-baked businesses and products. Even worse, the flood of capital led to enormous overcapacity, devastating entire industries.

We can only hope that the analogy ends there. The mid-nineteenth-century boom in railroads (and the closely related technologies of the steam engine and the telegraph) helped produce not only widespread industrial overcapacity but a surge in productivity. The combination set the stage for two solid decades of deflation. Although worldwide economic production continued to grow strongly between the mid-1870s and the mid-1890s, prices collapsed – in England, the dominant economic power of the time, price levels dropped 40%. In turn, business profits evaporated. Companies watched the value of their products erode while they were in the very process of making them. As the first worldwide depression took hold, economic malaise covered much of the globe. "Optimism about a future of indefinite progress gave way to uncertainty and a sense of agony," wrote historian D.S. Landes.

It's a very different world today, of course, and it would be dangerous to assume that history will repeat itself. But with companies struggling to boost profits and the entire world economy flirting with deflation, it would also be dangerous to assume it can't.

What About the Vendors?

Just a few months ago, at the 2003 World Economic Forum in Davos, Switzerland, Bill Joy, the chief scientist and cofounder of Sun Microsystems, posed what for him must have been a painful question: "What if the reality is that people have already bought most of the stuff they want to own?" The people he was talking about are, of course, businesspeople, and the stuff is information technology. With the end of the great buildout of the commercial IT infrastructure apparently at hand, Joy's question is one that all IT vendors should be asking themselves. There is good reason to believe that companies' existing IT capabilities are largely sufficient for their needs and, hence, that the recent and widespread sluggishness in IT demand is as much a structural as a cyclical phenomenon.

Even if that's true, the picture may not be as bleak as it seems for vendors, at least those with the foresight and skill to adapt to the new environment. The importance of infrastructural technologies to the day-to-day operations of business means that they continue to absorb large amounts of corporate cash long after they have become commodities – indefinitely, in many cases. Virtually all companies today continue to spend heavily on electricity and phone service, for example, and many manufacturers continue to spend a lot on rail transport. Moreover, the standardized nature of infrastructural technologies often leads to the establishment of lucrative monopolies and oligopolies.

Many technology vendors are already repositioning themselves and their products in response to the changes in the market. Microsoft's push to turn its Office software suite from a packaged good into an annual subscription service is a tacit acknowledgment that companies are losing their need – and their appetite – for constant upgrades. Dell has succeeded by exploiting the commoditization of the PC market and is now extending that strategy to servers, storage, and even services. (Michael Dell's essential genius has always been his unsentimental trust in the commoditization of information technology.) And many of the major suppliers of corporate IT, including Microsoft, IBM, Sun, and Oracle, are battling to position themselves as dominant suppliers of "Web services" – to turn themselves, in effect, into utilities. This war for scale, combined with the continuing transformation of IT into a commodity, will lead to the further consolidation of many sectors of the IT industry. The winners will do very well; the losers will be gone.

The Sprint to Commoditization

One of the most salient characteristics of infrastructural technologies is the rapidity of their installation, Spurred by massive investment, capacity soon skyrockets, leading to falling prices and, quickly, commoditization.

Railroad track worldwide, in thousands of kilometers

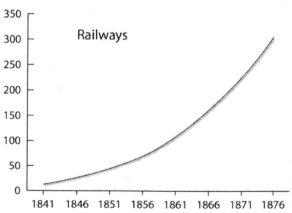

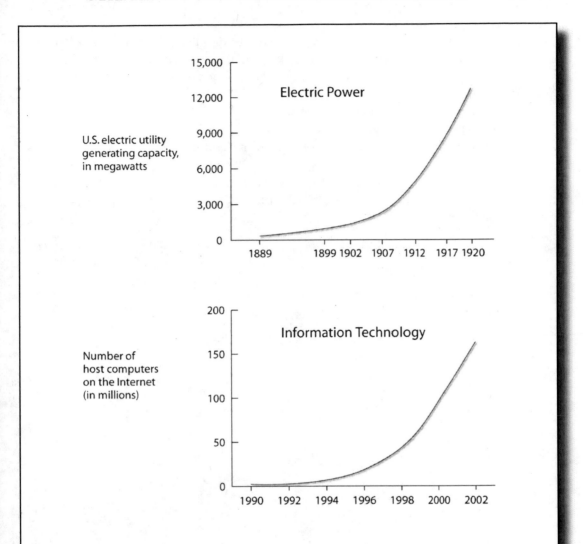

New Rules for IT Management

With the opportunities for gaining strategic advantage from information technology rapidly disappearing, many companies will want to take a hard look at how they invest in IT and manage their systems. As a starting point, here are three guidelines for the future:

Spend less. Studies show that the companies with the biggest IT investments rarely post the best financial results. As the commoditization of ITcontinues, the penalties for wasteful spending will only grow larger. It is getting much harder to achieve a competitive advantage through an IT investment, but it is getting much easier to put your business at a cost disadvantage.

Follow, don't lead. Moore's Law guarantees that the longer you wait to make an IT purchase, the more you'll get for your money. And waiting will decrease your risk of buying something technologically flawed or doomed to rapid obsolescence. In some cases, being on the cutting edge makes sense. But those cases are becoming rarer and rarer as IT capabilities become more homogenized.

Focus on vulnerabilities, not opportunities. It's unusual for a company to gain a competitive advantage through the distinctive use of a mature infrastructural technology, but even a brief disruption in the availability of the technology can be devastating. As corporations continue to cede control over their IT applications and networks to vendors and other third parties, the threats they face will proliferate. They need to prepare themselves for technical glitches, outages, and security breaches, shifting their attention from opportunities to vulnerabilities.

Does IT Matter? An HBR Debate

Every magazine has an ideal, or an idealized, reader. For *Harvard Business Review,* he or she is an executive of uncommon intelligence and curiosity: the brightest CEO you know or can imagine, perhaps. We like to pretend that our ideal reader has chartered us to prepare a briefing every month. On the agenda ,we've been told, should be three kinds of items.

First, our reader says, bring me important new ideas, research, or insights: "Boss, here's something you should know."

Second, bring me important eternal truths, rediscovered and refreshed: "Boss, here's something you shouldn't forget."

Third, bring me into the picture about important issues and arguments: "Boss, here's something you will want to know about."

New ideas, truths, and disputes: When we do our job well, HBR is a forum where you get some of each, and all of it is important. Nicholas G. Carr's "IT Doesn't Matter," published in the May 2003 issue, falls into the third category. It takes one side of an argument that's undeniably urgent and important to business leaders.

In 2000, nearly half of U.S. corporate capital spending went to information technology. Then the spending collapsed and the Nasdaq with it, and in every boardroom—and in every technology company—people began to wonder: What happened? What was that spending about? What's changed? What has not? And what do we do now? What is our technology strategy, and how does it affect our corporate strategy?

Forcefully, Carr argues that investments in IT, while profoundly important, are less and less likely to deliver a competitive edge to an individual company. "No one would dispute that information technology has become the backbone of commerce," Carr says. "The point is, however, that the technology's potential for differentiating one company from the pack – its strategic potential – inexorably diminishes as it becomes accessible and affordable to all."

Unsurprisingly, "IT Doesn't Matter" has generated an enormous amount of controversy. Our ideal reader wants that give-and-take, argument and counterargument, the better to understand the issues. Always in such cases, people are more likely to write to us when they disagree with an article's point of view than when they agree with it. Always in such cases, a few people mistake the argument. (In this instance, the most common misperception is that the article says that IT is dead and that it will not continue to be a source of dramatic, even transformational change. It doesn't say that. Instead, it says the odds are that the benefits of such changes will inure to whole industries rather than any one competitor. Instead of seeking advantage through technology, Carr argues, companies should manage IT defensively –watching costs and avoiding risks.)

And always in such cases, some very smart, thoughtful people present urgent, cogent, and forceful challenges to the article's conclusions.

We have received so many thoughtful letters that we have decided to publish them here, together with Carr's reply. That decision reflects – among other things – one way in which the ubiquity of IT has created new opportunities for us and for all publishers to interact with readers. It also reflects HBR's continuing commitment to offer readers a forum full of thoughtful voices, bringing you what's newly learned, what's fiercely argued, and what truly matters.

Thomas A. Stewart
Editor

Letter from John Seely Brown and John Hagel III

Nicholas Carr's article "IT Doesn't Matter" (May 2003) is an important, perhaps even seminal, piece. It effectively captures the zeitgeist among senior managers of large enterprises and gives eloquent voice to the backlash that has swept through management suites regarding IT's business value.

As Carr's article says, businesses have overestimated the strategic value of IT. They have significantly overspent on technology in the quest for business value. They need to manage large portions of their IT infrastructures more rigorously to reduce capital investment requirements and operating costs. As companies become more dependent on IT platforms for their day-to-day operations, they must focus on potential vulnerabilities and more aggressively manage for reliability and security. But such ideas are not inconsistent with the view that IT remains a profound catalyst for the creation of strategic differentiation.

In capturing today's management mood so effectively, Carr provides a valuable service. And yet his article is potentially dangerous, for it appears to endorse the notion that businesses should manage IT as a commodity input because the opportunities for strategic differentiation with IT have become so scarce. By giving voice to this perspective and making it so compelling, Carr is likely to perpetuate a misguided view.

The choice of article title is even more unfortunate. It may grab readers' attention, but it is misleading: Carr is not claiming that IT does not matter; rather, his main assertion is that IT is diminishing as a source of strategic differentiation. Unfortunately, given today's business climate, many readers will remember the article's title and forget its nuance.

The lesson to be learned from the past several decades is that IT by itself rarely, if ever, confers strategic differentiation. Yet, IT is inherently strategic because of its indirect effects—it creates possibilities and options that did not exist before. Companies that see, and act on, these possibilities before others do will continue to differentiate themselves in the marketplace and reap economic rewards. IT may become ubiquitous, but the insight required to harness its potential will not be so evenly distributed. Therein lies the opportunity for significant strategic advantage.

The experiences of the past several decades suggest three broad lessons regarding IT:

Extracting value from IT requires innovations in business practices. Companies that mechanically insert IT into their businesses without changing their practices for exploiting the new capabilities will only destroy IT's economic value. Unfortunately, all too many companies do this. For that reason, the research findings by Alinean and Forrester –that IT spending rarely correlates with superior financial results – are not surprising.

In October 2001, the McKinsey Global Institute published a study on "U.S. Productivity Growth, 1995–2000." That study was the first disciplined attempt to look at the correlation between IT investments and productivity by industry sector. The results were revealing. The study found a significant positive correlation between IT investments and productivity in only six out of 59 industries. The other 53 sectors, accounting for 70% of the economy, in aggregate saw negligible productivity improvements as a result of their IT investments.

Why only six industries? In each of these sectors, one or more companies introduced significant innovations in business practices to leverage their IT capabilities. This set into motion competitive pressures that forced other companies in the sector to implement comparable business practices. The classic example was retailing, where Wal-Mart innovated continuously around new generations of IT. Even as competitors adopted Wal- Mart's practices, the retailing giant focused on the next wave of innovations, preserving a significant productivity advantage (on the order of 40%) relative to competitors.

Significant opportunities for innovation continue to occur because advances in IT create possibilities not previously economically available. With few exceptions, companies have tended to think too narrowly about the possibilities. In particular, many companies have become locked into the view that IT can reduce transaction costs but then think of transaction costs as encompassing only the transfer of bits and data from one place to another. Viewed more broadly, transaction costs encompass such challenging business issues as the creation of meaning, the building of trust, and the development and dissemination of knowledge. These dimensions of transaction costs often represent significant bottlenecks to performance improvements and competitive advantage. Companies like Cisco in their e-learning initiatives are just beginning to explore the innovations in business practices required to exploit IT's potential for addressing such business challenges.

Companies also think too narrowly about IT's possibilities when they focus so heavily on business practices within the enterprise. In fact, many opportunities for business-practice innovations extend beyond the walls of the enterprise to include relationships with other companies. Rather than think in narrow transactional terms, as evidenced by the first wave of business-to-business marketplaces, executives would be far better advised to think in terms of opportunities to build long-term relationships with companies possessing complementary assets and capabilities. Companies like Li & Fung, with its orchestration model based on a loosely coupled approach to process management spanning thousands of companies, suggest opportunities for redefining relationships among companies and, in the process, creating significant differentiation.

In short, many executives have started to view IT as a commodity because they have not thought aggressively enough about how IT can bring about new business practices. The differentiation is not in IT itself but in the new practices it enables. IT does indeed matter. Although IT may be ubiquitous and increasingly less expensive, the insight and ability required for it to create economic value are in very short supply. It is far different from commodities like wheat and aluminum, where the processing operations are well understood and the economic advantage lies in being able to source the commodity at lower cost.

IT's economic impact comes from incremental innovations rather than "big bang" initiatives. In highlighting the significant opportunities for new business practices enabled by IT, we do not want to be misinterpreted as advocating big bang efforts to transform companies overnight. If we've learned one thing from the 1990s, it's that big bang, IT driven initiatives rarely produce expected returns; they are complicated and expensive, take a long time to implement, and are fraught with risk. Rather than create economic value, more often than not they destroy it.

The companies most successful in harnessing IT's power typically proceed in waves of relatively short-term (often six to 12 months) operating initiatives designed to test and refine specific innovations in business practices. Changing business practices creates unintended consequences. By "chunking up" innovations in business practices and tying these initiatives to explicit operating performance metrics, management can create tighter feedback loops and accelerate the learning process. If done right, these innovations can also reduce the financial risks by generating near-term returns that can help fund subsequent waves of operating initiatives. Politically, this kind of incremental approach, with its relentless focus on tangible near-term returns, also helps deepen organizational support for new business practices while neutralizing potential opposition.

The strategic impact of IT investments comes from the cumulative effect of sustained initiatives to innovate business practices in the near term. If IT's economic value comes from very tactical near-term initiatives to innovate business practices, aren't we in fact conceding that IT has lost its power to provide strategic differentiation? Aren't we just saying that IT can provide tactical advantage that will be quickly copied by competitors? Far from it. The strategic differentiation emerges over time, based less on the specific innovations in business practices at any point in time and much more on the ability to continually innovate around IT's evolving capabilities.

To understand this point, it is essential to differentiate the characteristics of IT as an infrastructure technology relative to the variety of other infrastructure technologies cited by Carr – steam engines, railroads, electricity, and telephones. In each of those prior areas, the underlying technology burst forth in one relatively concentrated innovation. While the technology's performance continued to improve after it was introduced, the rate of improvement was far more modest and reached a point of diminishing returns much sooner than we have seen in the decades since the introduction of digital technology. Thus, the ability to continually innovate business practices around these technologies also reached a period of diminishing returns. Another result was that these prior generations of technology produced a dominant design or architecture relatively quickly – for example, the standardization of railway gauges or alternating-current specifications. The emergence of these dominant designs or architectures catalyzed the various industry shakeouts and helped to further standardize the use of these technologies.

IT thus far has followed a very different path. Improvements in processing power, storage capacity, and bandwidth have continued at a rapid and sustained pace. Indeed, these performance improvements have had a multiplicative effect, coming together, for example, to form entirely new ways of storing, distributing, and accessing data. Not only are smart things getting smarter, but this technology is also being used to make dumb things smarter through such extensions as MEMS, RFID, and telematics. IT is also extending its reach to biological organisms, redefining the ways we diagnose, treat, and even design life forms.

This sustained pace and expanding range of digital technology innovation continues to precipitate fundamental new opportunities for thinking about how we organize such technology. We are now on the cusp of a shift to distributed service architectures that will unleash entirely new capabilities at least as significant as the shift from proprietary and centralized mainframe architectures to more distributed client-server architectures. Far from settling down into a dominant design or architecture, IT has crashed through several generations of architectures and continues to generate new ones. In fact, the emerging service-oriented architectures enable a kind of radical incrementalism that transcends what one might expect from simple incrementalism. Coupled with a strategy focused on both short-term wins and long-term goals, this new incrementalism is a source of competitive advantage.

The underlying technology components may be widely and cheaply available, but the skills required to organize them into high-value architectures are still in very short supply, and a new generation of skills must be developed with each new generation of architecture. These new architectures amplify the possibilities enabled by the performance improvements in the underlying technology components.

The gap between IT's potential and business's realization of that potential has not narrowed. Instead, it has steadily widened over the past several decades. This gap creates enormous instability in the business world. Wherever there is so much potential for instability, there is also fertile ground for new strategies.

To further amplify the effect of these performance improvements in terms of real business-practice innovation and to convert tactical advantage into strategic advantage, something else is required. Companies need to align themselves around a long-term view of the challenges and opportunities brought about by IT. Senior managers need a shared but high-level view of the kinds of markets they are likely to be operating in and the kinds of companies they will need to become if they are to continue creating economic value. This long-term view helps to focus and prioritize near-term innovations in business practices, thereby helping to build a sustainable strategic advantage across multiple waves of initiatives. It is exactly this kind of long-term view that guides Dell and Wal-Mart in their ongoing use of IT to create strategic advantage.

Without this view, even the most aggressive near-term incremental initiatives run the risk of becoming dispersed over too many fronts. The continuing performance improvements of IT create far more possibilities than any company can or should pursue. The temptation in this kind of environment is to launch too many initiatives. The result is that few, if any, of the near-term initiatives produce the expected results. Without focusing on the long-term, companies will have difficulty building momentum across multiple waves of operating initiatives. Each new wave responds to the events of the moment rather than driving toward a common destination. The focus remains entirely on near-term initiatives rather than on building a more sustained capability to innovate and leverage IT's new capabilities. Short-term tactical advantage remains just that–tactical and transitory. In such a world, it is easy to see why management could come to believe that IT does not produce significant strategic differentiation.

Paradoxically, technology vendors themselves are somewhat responsible for the widespread belief that IT doesn't produce significant strategic differentiation. For too long, they have built their businesses around big bang, IT-centric selling propositions. Rather than help companies understand that IT is only a tool, technology vendors have tended to present it as a panacea. "Buy this technology and all your problems will be solved." It is a seductive proposition. Rather than focusing on the enormous challenge of innovating in business practices and creating the discipline required to generate economic value from these innovations, vendors have convinced many companies that signing a purchase order would deliver the required value. They even managed to convince companies, for a while, that they needed to buy a lot of the technology because the only way to stay competitive was through massive IT implementations. When the anticipated results didn't materialize, the backlash began to gather force in executive suites. Executives swing from one extreme to the other. If IT doesn't solve all their business problems, then it must not matter, at least in terms of strategic value. We still need it to run our business, but let's buy as little as we can and squeeze the vendors as much as we can. It has never been true that IT matters in isolation. It only matters in the context of a concerted effort to innovate based on new possibilities and opportunities created by the technology. Then it matters –and will continue to–a lot.

That's a far more difficult message for IT vendors to communicate to customers. It's an even more difficult message for the vendors to execute against. It means changing their economic model, selling model, organizational model, and product strategies in fundamental and very painful ways. Yet, the alternative for technology vendors is to cope with the growing belief that IT really doesn't matter, at least in terms of its potential for strategic differentiation. In the end, that will be a far more painful world for them to confront. It will also be a tragedy for businesses that continue to miss the opportunities IT creates.

John Seely Brown, *Former Chief Scientist, Xerox, Palo Alto, California*
John Hagel III, *Management Consultant and Author, Burlingame, California*

Letter from F. Warren McFarlan and Richard L. Nolan

In no other area is it more important to have a sense of what you *don't* know than it is in IT management. The most dangerous advice to CEOs has come from people who either had no idea of what they did not know, or from those who pretended to know what they didn't. Couple not knowing that you don't know with fuzzy logic, and you have the makings of Nicholas Carr's article.

Carr's examples of railroads and electric power played out over 80 years, (not 40, as he suggests), turning society, business organizations, and lifestyles inside out. The deeper societal impacts came during the second 40 years, as society's insights on how to use the technology changed. It is worth noting that although these technologies mutated significantly (for trains, it meant moving from 15 miles an hour to 80 miles an hour), the mutation was on a totally different and much smaller scale than IT's.

The cost performance of IT technologies over the first 40 years changed by roughly 10 to the seventh, and for the foreseeable future will continue to evolve at the same rate. That is in sharp contrast to a train, which after 80 years moved six times faster than it had in the earlier period. This is impressive, but not nearly as dramatic as a computer produced in 2000, which runs 10 million times faster than a 1960s' computer.

Carr's graph on information technology stands as a subject lesson for Darrell Huff's well-known book *How to Lie with Statistics*. Carr's chart would look very different if he had tracked the number of MIPS or CPU cycles on the network from 1990 to 2002. Even using a log scale on the vertical axis would be barely enough to tilt a vertical straight line enough to create something resembling the curves of the other two schematics in Carr's article. With this explosion of cost-effectiveness has come the ability to do things truly differently. American Hospital Supply's distribution software and American Airlines' SABRE reservation system are examples of victories in past technologies. The firms were the first in their industries to see technology's transforming potential, they had the courage to invest in its performance, and they used it to gain a significant competitive edge. It is naive to assume that other sharply discontinuous technologies will not offer similar transformation opportunities in the future.

In our view, the most important thing that the CEO and senior management should understand about IT is its associated economics. Driven by Moore's Law, those evolving economics have enabled every industry's transaction costs to decrease continually, resulting in new economics for the firm and creating the feasibility of products and services not possible in the past. The economics of financial transactions have continually dropped from dollars to cents. New entrants have joined many industries and have focused on taking strategic advantage of IT's associated economics. Company boundaries have become permeable, organic, and global in scope through IT networks and the Internet.

As the pace of doing business increases, the CEO and senior management team must be aware of how IT can change rules and assumptions about competition. The economics of conducting business will likewise continue to improve –providing opportunities for businesses to expand the customer value proposition by providing more intangible information-based services. For example, the automobile value proposition continues to expand with technology that continuously senses road conditions and applies the appropriate wheel traction and suspension system pressures.

CEO and senior management must understand that historical constraints of every kind continue to be knocked off IT because it is a "universal information-processing machine." Before e-mail and the Internet, the cost of communications was seen as limiting IT's wider use. Packet switching was invented as a way to digitize voice, data, and video in a matter that enabled digital computers (and its associated economics) to communicate, and the cost of communication sharply and suddenly dropped. Similar situations have transpired with the advent of digitized photography, use of radio frequencies for various handheld IT appliances, and the development of such products as elevators that call in to the service center or to a computer that automatically dispatches collective software or people when a part or system is about to fail. Often, only the senior management team's imagination limits new IT-based opportunities.

Our research suggests the following:

New technologies will continue to give companies the chance to differentiate themselves by service, product feature, and cost structure for some time to come. The first mover takes a risk and gains a temporary advantage (longer if there are follow-on possibilities). The fast follower is up against less risk but also has to recover lost ground. Charles Schwab versus Merrill Lynch and Walgreens versus CVS are examples of this playing out over the past decade. Our advice to the CEO is to look at IT use through several different lenses. One lens should be focused on improving cost savings and efficiencies. Another should be focused on the incremental improvement of organizational structure, products, and services. Still another should be focused on the creation of strategic advantage through extending competitive scope, partnerships (customers and other parties), the changing of the rules of competition, and the provision of new IT-based services to extend the customer value proposition.

Unless nurtured and evolved, IT enabled competitive applications, like many competitive advantages, don't endure. Even historic strategic systems like American Hospital Supply's (after a decade of financial malnourishment) may wind up turning into a strategic liability. Others, however, like American Airlines' SABRE have shown extraordinary robustness and have permitted the survival of otherwise doomed organizations.

Evaluating these opportunities as well as thinking through their implications and timing, is vitally important, non-boring work. The new technologies will allow new things to be transformed in nonlinear ways. Radio-frequency identification devices for grocery stores, smart cards, and automated ordering systems for hospital physicians are all examples of new process targets that technologies will soon address. In the more distant future we will see the improved creation of drugs and treatments through the ability to rapidly and more deeply analyze huge databases. Understanding the potential and then deciding when the time is right to seize these transformative applications will be neither routine nor boring for the CEO or CIO.

Grid computing, standardization of components, and open systems, far from stifling differentiation, provide a stable platform to build on and offer new ways of differentiating, either by cost structure, product, or service. Just as literacy stimulated innovation, so do open systems and grids.

Outsourcing the commodity infrastructure is a great way to control costs, build competence, and free up resources, which can be used to combine data bits in creative ways to add value. Relatively bulletproof operational reliability will be a key part of the price of success. Back-office or server farms, help desks, and network operations will be outsourced to specialists to attain this reliability (at rock-bottom costs). Packages like SAP further help remove commodity maintenance activities and allow firms to better analyze customer information and provide service at the sharp end. The package of skills needed inside an organization is changing very fast for competition in the information age.

The jobs of the CTO and CIO are and will be of unparalleled importance in the decades ahead. Max Hopper of American Airlines and Paul Strassmann of Kraft and NASA are not the last of a dying breed of dinosaurs, but prototypes of the leadership skills needed for survival.

If you take 1955 (with the IBM 701) as the start date and use 80 years as a technology cycle, 2035 may not be far off the mark for playing much of this out. Even then, the special recombinant nature of this technology makes us uncomfortable calling an end date. We wish Carr were right, because everyone's golf handicap could then improve. Unfortunately, the evidence is all to the contrary.

F. Warren McFarlan, *Albert H. Gordon Professor of Business Administration, Harvard Business School, Boston*
Richard L. Nolan, *William Barclay Harding Professor of Business Administration, Harvard Business School, Boston*

Letter from Jason Hittleman

I largely agree with Nicholas Carr's suggestions on how companies should respond to the unbearable reality that IT is becoming more of a commodity. But why does Carr suggest that IT management should become boring? Are leadership tasks such as managing risk and reining in costs any less engaging or challenging than seeking competitive advantage is?

Competitive advantage should never be the sole objective of IT. Rather, managing costs and assessing risk must become standard objectives as well. By focusing on systems and processes, more so than on just technologies, and by coupling the suggestions outlined in the article with an approach that embraces the mission of the company, IT management can remain challenging and rewarding.

IT will always matter–it will just matter in different ways now. IT must continue to support the business – not just through the logical application of technologies but also through the logical application of common sense.

Jason Hittleman, *IT Director, RKA Petroleum Companies, Romulus, Michigan*

Letter from Paul A. Strassmann

Nicholas Carr pronounces information technology strategically irrelevant to businesses and recommends adoption of the following policies: Cut IT budgets; do not invest in information technology innovations; invest only after others have succeeded (follow, do not lead); delay IT investments because prices are dropping and everything will be less expensive later; refocus from seeking opportunities to managing vulnerabilities and risks; disregard innovative offerings because vendors are seeking added revenues and are therefore suspect; and delay innovation as the preferred way for cutting IT costs. These recommendations are a departure from policies that have been pursued for the past 50 years. Therefore, each of the assertions Carr makes to support them warrants a commentary.

Assertion: IT has lost its strategic value. Carr argues that IT is no longer strategic because it has ceased to be a scarce good, and he contends that profit margins on IT-related innovations will consequently disappear. He does not support this argument with research findings (except for a reference to my own research and a misunderstood example from the Alinean Corporation). He bases his conclusions entirely on his reasoning, by analogy, that IT must follow the patterns that arose as businesses adopted steam engines, railroads, telephones, electric generators, and internal combustion motors. But any proof that rests entirely on analogies is flawed. This technique was used to uphold medieval dogma, and it delayed the advancement of science by centuries.

Carr's logic is defective because his examples deal exclusively with capital-intensive goods. Capital investments in machinery do indeed exhibit diminishing returns as markets saturate and the difference between marginal costs and marginal revenues disappears, but information goods are not subject to such effects. The marginal cost of information goods – especially of software, which now accounts for the dominant share of information technology costs – does not rise with increased scale. It drops asymptotically toward zero. Therefore, any firm that can steadily reduce marginal costs by deploying IT can make information technology investments enormously profitable and can generate a rising strategic value.

Assertion: IT is a commodity that does not offer a competitive distinction and therefore does not provide a competitive advantage. It is true that Microsoft desktops running on Intel processors have become widespread, but they account for less than 12% of IT budgets, and that number is declining. Most IT products are diverse – they certainly are not commodities. And while many business processes do rely on standardized desktops, are those processes therefore doomed to uniformity? In other words, does partial standardization wipe out opportunities for gaining competitive advantage? The evidence does not support such a conclusion.

Competitive advantage is not the result of personal computers. It is the result of effective management by skilled and highly motivated people. Since 1982 I have shown (in numerous publications) that firms using identical information technologies and spending comparable amounts on IT display an enormous variability in profitability. My research, now confirmed by other investigators, has demonstrated that profitability and IT spending are unrelated, even if identical technologies are used.

Assertion: Because IT is an infrastructural technology that is easily acquired and copied, it cannot offer a competitive advantage. Easy availability of information technology makes it increasingly valuable. E-mail, fax, and cell phones gain in utility as they become more widely used, because they can be acquired on attractive terms. I have spent 40 years of my career implementing information technologies; for the first 30 years, that was a great pain. The technology was expensive, faulty, insecure, hard to manage, and unstable. I finally see the advent of an era in which low-cost ownership of information technologies is possible. This will be accomplished through services in which the vendors assume most of the risks of failure while increasing ease of use for billions of people.

Carr's advice to back off from information technologies just as they emerge from a long gestation period is mistimed and abortive. Information technology must be easily acquired and made available to everyone so that the global community can increase the standard of living through easier communications and lower-cost business transactions. Widespread availability creates new business opportunities.

Assertion: The influence of IT will henceforth be macroeconomic and not a means for competitive differentiation. The proposition that IT benefits will flow to consumers and not to firms is a contradiction. Sustainable profits materialize when benefits accrue to customers. There are as yet enormous gains in value to be delivered in health, education, entertainment, business services, and especially government. Extending the benefits of the global division of labor and the inclusion of billions of new consumers into the global marketplace will generate trillions of dollars of new revenues. Enabling the global marketplace to function effectively will require enormous new IT investments by individual firms. Surely there will be millions of enterprises that will be able to take advantage of such opportunities. The lower entry costs for using the power of information technologies will make that feasible. Carr completely disregards the explosive growth of small businesses, a development made possible by the Internet. Information technology is a killer of bureaucracies and a reducer of overhead expenses; those qualities increase its microeconomic viability. Asserting that benefits will accrue only to the economy at large and not to individual firms is a prescription for opting out of the information-based competitive races in the years to come.

Assertion: IT is primarily a transport technology, and because it is open to everyone, it offers no advantage. This proposition is a misunderstanding of what IT is all about. Message transport is *not* the primary reason why organizations deploy IT. Information technology adds value mainly by improving the management of information intelligence and collaboration among individuals, groups, and organizations. The transport function is essential, but IT's importance as a conduit is only tertiary. The value is in the message itself, not in the means of conveyance!

Information technologies now provide the primary means for extending the value of a firm's knowledge capital. They help companies manage the exploding accumulation of scientific, research, customer, engineering, property, and intellectual assets. Computers are the repositories of intelligence about customers, suppliers, and products; those repositories constitute the most valuable knowledge assets for any firm that realizes returns greater than its cost of financial capital. It is noteworthy that information technology is now recognized as the means for waging information warfare – a term that I apply not only to the military but also to commercial confrontations.

I have shown in published articles how and why firms' knowledge capital is now worth more than the assets reported on conventional financial statements. I have shown how people become enormously empowered when aided by information technologies because these tools magnify their ability to perform complex tasks. By trivializing information technologies as electronic messengers, Carr would prevent organizations from understanding how to deploy IT in such a way that it can be the weapon of choice in competitive contests.

Assertion: IT functions will be homogenized, and proprietary applications are therefore doomed. Citing the proliferation of off-the-shelf, standard applications, such as Microsoft Office, Carr predicts that information practices will march inexorably toward homogeneity. In such an environment of sameness, he says, no companies will be able to realize competitive gains.

The use of a standard software package does not doom an organization to homogeneity that destroys value. I suspect that Carr used the same software to write his essay that I did to write this critique, yet we have arrived at opposite conclusions! I consider the standardization of communication protocols, Web services, database languages, and applications to be a value-enhancing development, not a value detractor. I am particularly in favor of open systems that will make systems integration – now an enormous, resource-sapping burden – easy and financially attractive. Standards spare IT executives from unceasing difficulties in assuring the interoperability of routine business processes. With standards in place, the IT staff can finally concentrate on what is indeed value enhancing for the enterprise, such as applications that reflect the firm's distinctive characteristics and allow it to share information easily with customers and suppliers. Applications that were completely custom-designed in the past – and that Carr praises – inhibited the economic contributions of IT.

Assertion: Corporations will adopt generic applications; business processes will therefore be uniform and without competitive advantage. This assertion can be contradicted by anyone who has had experience with one-code-fits-all "enterprise" software suites that claim to deliver answers to most business-systems problems. Even the most tightly controlled generic application suite (SAP's enterprise resource planning application) can deliver completely different results for look-alike firms.

For routine business processes, generic applications can be useful in reducing the total cost of ownership of computer systems. But such applications have also been known to destroy firms that have attempted to squeeze unique company processes into generic molds. Carr's prediction that generic applications will take over is not supported by firms' rising reluctance to install comprehensive enterprise solutions. In fact, by insisting on data and protocol interoperability, firms are seeking greater freedom to combine applications from a growing diversity of software offerings.

Assertion: Existing IT capabilities are largely sufficient for corporate needs. It is hubris to assert that we have already attained the pinnacle of what is ultimately achievable. The history of that assertion is a history of failures. The Chinese burned their fleet when they thought nothing further could be gained from overseas trade. The leaders of the Soviet Union retained their bankrupt central planning system because they considered it perfect for managing the economy.

Corporations are confronting increased uncertainty about markets, competition, resources, employee attitudes, and the impact of legislation. The corporate environment requires more complex coordination than ever before, and there is less time for taking corrective measures. As a result, there is a need for more and better information technologies. Carr's view that the time has come to arrest further IT developments and take a static posture is a prescription for inaction as challenges keep rising.

Assertion: Widespread adoption of best-practices software makes IT-based advantages disappear for everyone. The dissemination of information about best business practices is indeed gaining, and competitors are therefore getting smarter and faster. But Carr's view– that wins cannot be sustainable if everyone has access to the same means for engaging in contests – disregards the dynamics of competition. The proliferation of knowledge about how to design ever faster sailing boats has jacked up the cost of participating and increased the difficulty of winning, but it has not discouraged races. The dissemination of business best practices means survival today requires speed and innovation – and greater adoption of information technologies. The arrival of a new information- based best practice is usually seen by the more aggressive leaders as a signal to commence yet another round of more expensive competition with more, not less, IT.

Assertion: IT is arriving at the end of its growth cycle and is reaching saturation. After 50 years of cyclical growth, there is not a shred of evidence that IT developments have reached a plateau, as did innovations in industrial-age machinery. Physical mechanics impose limits on the size and performance of locomotives, turbines, airplanes, refrigerators, and trucks; there are no such confinements to information technologies, as far as we can tell. Software can endow computing devices with unrestricted variability in features and functions. The capability of a software-enriched global network has no boundaries. The current cyclical correction to the excesses of the past decade is a crucible for generating more and better innovation.

Assertion: IT risks now exceed advantages, requiring shifts in executive attention.

The need to pay more attention to IT risks is indisputable, but I do not agree that the risks exceed the advantages. Carr advises executives to adopt a reclusive posture – to withdraw from the search for new opportunities. He recommends pursuing cost reductions through cutting off IT instead of searching for opportunities in the steady stream of new ideas.

I favor cost cutting, especially for any bloated computing capacity that was acquired in a frenzy of hype without an enterprise architecture or alignment with a strategic plan. And I share Carr's concerns about information security, network reliability, and systems corruption. But cutting off innovative investments is not the way to address those problems. The cure for most of the so-called "legacy" systems is radical innovation, such as shifting the accountability for systems performance to vendors, who will then have to face up to the responsibility of delivering reliable and robust applications. I have examined such options. An examination of a large collection of applications shows that the most financially attractive way of dealing with existing risks is to replace the systems. Instead of feeding the increasingly costly IT infrastructure and throwing money at rising software maintenance costs, companies should be ready to engage in yet another IT investment cycle to replace old systems.

• • •

Carr's assertions and recommendations could inhibit the most innovative and value-creating means available for increasing the economic benefits to enterprises and customers. Information technologies are too important to be pronounced irrelevant.

Paul A. Strassmann, *Executive Advisor, NASA; Former CIO of General Foods, Kraft, Xerox, the Department of Defense, and NASA*

Letter from Marianne Broadbent, Mark McDonald, and Richard Hunter

Nicholas Carr's well-written article takes the view that IT is now like other infrastructures and that, on average, the companies that are the biggest investors in IT are not the most successful in terms of business performance. He contends that firms should now focus on carefully managing costs and risks and not get carried away with IT's strategic role.

Carr is correct that hardware and network connectivity are commodity businesses and that some IT infrastructure services have evolved into commodity services. But the article misses a big part of the story. IT does matter, but not because of hardware or even standard commercial software. It is because the intelligent and innovative application of information solves business problems and creates customer value at high speed, low cost, and the right scale. To put it simply, it's not about the box; it's about what's inside the box.

Carr is right that the simple possession of infrastructure technology was for a time a source of competitive advantage. In the 1970s, the Dallas Cowboys' Tex Schram used a computer to manage information on NFL draft choices, assess the strengths of other football teams, and perform additional tasks that increased the Cowboys' ability to use information competitively. But the advantage disappeared when other teams began using computers. The source of competitive advantage shifted from simply having a computer to knowing how to use it.

Carr's examples are of companies looking for competitive advantage from the intrinsic performance characteristics of the hardware. In the case of American Hospital Supply, the characteristic was connectivity; at American Airlines, it was management of large amounts of complex data. In high tech, whenever you rely on hardware capability as a competitive technology, it's only a matter of time before others catch up.

The differentiation is about information, business processes, and applications. Sustainable advantage comes from consistently delivering greater value to customers. This comes from the "information" in information technology – that is, it comes from better understanding the customer, applying that understanding to your products, services, and processes, and integrating these to deliver on an improved value proposition.

That's what Wal-Mart and Dell have done. They have continuously used information better and with greater alignment to their value proposition. It's true that these companies have also continuously reinvested in new hardware and software platforms. But the sheer scale of their investment in infrastructure isn't the most important factor. Why have competitors been unable to copy Wal-Mart's and Dell's successes? The answer lies in large part in Wal-Mart's and Dell's ability to integrate IT into business processes – their "benefit conversion" ability.

It has been known for many years that the biggest investors in IT don't get the most value from the technologies. It is a key message in the Weill and Broadbent book *Leveraging the New Infrastructure: How Market Leaders Capitalize on Information Technology* (Harvard Business School Press, 1998) and in much subsequent work. What makes the difference is a set of benefit conversion factors that influence how well investments in IT-enabled business initiatives are turned into real business value. These factors include clear decision rights, accountability for IT-related decisions, integrated business and technology planning and execution, and the existence and reinforcement of strong collaborative behaviors. Many of these are not about IT as such but about effective executive processes, effective accountabilities, and business focus.

The major messages we have been giving CIOs over the past two years have been that they should manage costs and risks aggressively and work with business colleagues to design IT governance thoughtfully. Beyond that, as in any business area, executives must understand the need for risk-managed innovation.

Innovation through electronically enabled services, processes, and products has only just begun. As in the past, the benefits will go to firms where the business focus is clear and disciplined and where there is well-informed and integrated decision making across the organization. The danger is that by scanting the fantastic potential for innovation that lies ahead in IT, Carr will lead executives to focus only on controlling IT costs. That is a necessary discipline, but it is not the route to real business advantage.

Marianne Broadbent, *Group Vice President and Gartner Fellow, Global Head of Research, Executive Programs, Gartner*
Mark McDonald, *Vice President and Research Director, Executive Programs, Gartner*
Richard Hunter, *Vice President and Gartner Fellow, Executive Programs, Gartner*

Letter from Bruce Skaistis

In "IT Doesn't Matter," Nicholas Carr is essentially issuing a warning: Organizations need to get realistic about what IT can and cannot do for them. In spite of all the hype, wireless systems and other exciting new computer technologies aren't going to create lasting strategic advantages.

I also think Carr is trying to help us learn from the mistakes we made during the late 1990s, when companies were making huge investments in e-business initiatives in an attempt to achieve competitive and strategic advantages. Many of those investments never produced significant benefits–many of the initiatives were never completed. With the benefit of hindsight, Carr is telling us most of those gigantic efforts were never going to deliver real strategic advantage, even if they had been successful.

IT does matter, and organizations should do the following to make sure their IT efforts and resources continue to matter:

Aim your IT efforts and resources at helping the business achieve its strategic objectives. Use IT to optimize and streamline critical business processes; speed up access to accurate information about operations, customers, and competitors; and integrate systems with customers and suppliers. Establish an active, effective IT management or governance structure, so leaders companywide can participate in establishing technology priorities, allocating resources, and monitoring performance.

Focus on using IT to respond quickly to changing conditions and requirements. Everything in business today has to be done faster than ever, and everything is subject to immediate change. Therefore, IT decisions have to be made more quickly. Put critical IT initiatives at the top of the priority list. And slot them on a fast track; they need to be completed in the shortest time possible and updated frequently. (After all, your competitors are probably just a few steps behind.)

Focus on optimizing the cost effectiveness and performance of IT resources. Despite the fact that IT investments are typically among the largest a company makes, IT resources haven't always been under the same pressure as other functional areas to improve overall corporate performance and reduce costs. Now that some of the IT mystique has been eliminated, corporate IT has to play by the same rules as everyone else. That means refocusing the entire company on the importance of IT performance and cost effectiveness; creating new IT management structures to monitor performance and cost effectiveness; consolidating resources; and streamlining processes.

Focus on minimizing IT risks. Carr rightfully concludes that minimizing IT risks is a critical issue for all companies. Almost every day there is a new story about a major company or government agency having their networks hacked or their Web sites attacked. Every company should have some of its most talented people worrying about how to manage its IT efforts and outsourcing relationships; protect its networks, systems, and information; and mitigate other IT risks.

In a very straightforward way, Carr has put a stake in the heart of the misdirected thinking about IT that flourished in the free-spending 1990s. It's time for enterprises to be realistic about IT's role in their future. IT can produce significant strategic and competitive benefits for an organization—but only when it is used effectively.

Bruce Skaistis, *President, eGlobal CIO, Tulsa, Oklahoma*

Letter from Vladimir Zwass

Two of the other articles in your May 2003 issue best refute Nicholas Carr's claim that "IT Doesn't Matter." As Gary Loveman describes in "Diamonds in the Data Mine," Harrah's Entertainment "has outplayed its competition" by basing its deep service orientation on how valuable its different kinds of customers are. The firm determines this value by mining the multifaceted and voluminous transactional information in its database. This is a textbook example of the strategic deployment of information technology to gain competitive advantage. Daniel Corsten and Nirmalya Kumar report in their Forethought article," Profits in the Pie of the Beholder," that the suppliers that comprehensively adopt the IT-based "efficient consumer response" practices in their relationships with Sainsbury's Supermarkets attain higher levels of economic performance than do their peers. This is an excellent example of the successful use of interorganizational systems for competitive advantage.

The hardware and software components of information technology do indeed provide the infrastructure for data storage, communication, and processing. This basic aspect of IT is certainly being commoditized. However, as these and other examples show, information systems can be embedded in a company's organizational and interorganizational processes and combined inextricably with other capabilities and assets to produce superior performance. Dell's pull-based order processing and Wal-Mart's supplier-relationship management come to mind. The implementation of these IT-based systems does not come cheaply and requires continual retargeting, yet it underlies the success of many firms.

Vladimir Zwass, *Distinguished Professor of Computer Science and MIS, Fairleigh Dickinson University, Teaneck, New Jersey, zwass@fdu.edu*

Letter from Mark S. Lewis

I agree with Nicholas Carr that the competitive edge gained by companies through IT in the past was not due to the fact that they had IT and others did not. It was due to *how* they used it, to the innovative business processes and models they created around new information technologies. Now, Carr tells us, best practices are being built into the infrastructure itself. He writes off any further strategic differentiation by arguing that IT is like other "infrastructure technologies" that lost their competitive potential once they became "accessible and affordable to all."

Carr's historical analogies to other infrastructure technologies are not convincing. Information technology has infinite and constantly expanding functionality, while Carr's other technologies – steam engines, railroads, electricity, telephones – have narrow functionality.

Electricity, for example, is simply a source of energy; it hasn't changed much since we found a way to harness it. And it can, and probably will, be replaced by another source of energy. Unlike electricity, IT is very different from what it was 30 or even ten years ago. The technologies used for processing, storing, and transporting information continue to expand. Also growing is the demand for IT, with more businesses and types of organizations, more processes and activities, and more and more consumers at home and on the go in need of its productivity-enhancing functions. Should we believe Carr, who says that the build-out is over, or should we listen to Alan Greenspan, who argues that "there are still significant opportunities for firms to upgrade the quality of their technology and with it the level of productivity"? Or perhaps we should listen to genomics expert Craig Venter, who says that at least a decade or two will go by before computing can catch up with the current needs of biological investigation. Or maybe we should observe the millions of businesses and people around the world who are currently without affordable access to IT.

The key difference between IT and Carr's other "infrastructure technologies" is that the latter perform functions that lie outside human capabilities. By contrast, much of IT mirrors and amplifies the brain's key information-handling activities: processing, storage, and transmission. In addition, IT is a tool that automates and facilitates activities that otherwise would be done manually. Strategic advantage comes from how we apply IT, the unique and differentiating ways in which we marry information technologies with our intellectual capital: our business models, our organizational cultures, our creativity.

IT never mattered. What matters are the people who invent information technologies and who deploy and use them. Like any other human endeavor, IT has its share of failures, foibles, and fads. Computer scientist Michael Dertouzos reminded us that "IT acts like a magnifying lens, amplifying management's strengths but also its weaknesses." Carr's advice to avoid "waste and sloppiness" applies to any investment or purchase we make. A few years of over-investment followed by a few years of under-investment due to general economic and psychological conditions cannot change the nature of information technologies nor the industry built around them.

In my job, I talk with a lot of business executives and IT managers around the world. These conversations paint a very different future from the one Carr predicts. Rather than "ceding control" to a few large IT utilities guaranteed to use their monopoly status to raise profits and squash innovation, the executives I've spoken with are demanding more choice, more flexibility, and more advanced IT. They, unlike Carr, do not confuse the way they buy IT – increasingly moving toward a consumption- based model –with a lack of strategic importance.

In the next generation of IT, there can be no compromises. The use of IT is analogous to innovations in transportation, not power utilities. Common standards like roads and airports exist, but the cars we choose to drive and our methods of travel are based on individual preference. IT utilities will exist, but businesses will derive unique benefits from how they leverage specific technologies.

The greatest improvements in IT economics have come when customers were able to take control from "full-solution" providers and utilize the most cost-effective technology applicable for their needs. There is no going back. In the foreseeable future, customers will require the simplicity and affordability of complete IT solutions but will still want to be creative and use their brains to do more with IT and, yes, gain competitive advantage. I just think of walking into our living room and telling my kids that we now have a "TV utility" and the only channel we get is C-SPAN. I don't think they would consider this a step forward.

Mark S. Lewis, *Executive Vice President of New Ventures, Chief Technology Officer, EMC Corporation, Hopkinton, Massachusetts*

Letter from Tom Pisello

How a company manages its information technology – aligning investments with core business goals – is more strategic now than ever. Nicholas Carr's article "IT Doesn't Matter" draws attention to the very heart of the question CIOs and CFOs struggle with most: "What's most important when it comes to IT investments? "With dollars being scrutinized, the question merits closer examination.

In specific market segments and over the long term, it is true that companies spending frugally on IT are demonstrating superior overall results. But dig deeper and you'll find that there is no consistent correlation between IT spending levels and financial performance; two companies investing the same amounts in identical technologies will yield vastly different results.

What does this mean? What a company invests in, and how well it is applied to improve business practices, counts far more than how much is spent.

On the flip side, the worst-performing companies – those delivering the lowest return on shareholder investment –are equally penurious in their IT investment. Our research indicates that this laggardly group spends well below the industry average of 3.7% of revenue on IT (as do the top performers).

Examination of industry averages reveals certain best practices of companies deriving strategic impact from IT investments; one of these is the ability to quickly adapt plans to shifting market conditions. Best-performing companies have been able to scale back spending in this slow economy. When and if a shift occurs back toward favoring innovation, these same companies are likely to be adept at scaling back up.

Unfortunately, commoditization of technologies does not translate into making the best

IT implementations easily replicable. That's because every organization has unique needs and priorities. However, one trend in particular holds great promise: Cheap, standards-based hardware and software are the single biggest driver of innovation, precisely because the heavy lifting can now be focused on activities that deliver much more value. (From databases, for instance, has sprung the promise of truly individualized customer contact; from the rudiments of factory planning come supply chains that can shift production within days of changes in customer demand or of geopolitical turmoil.)

Information technology is expected to manage companies' most vital and valuable intellectual assets and is the only tool companies have to turn this knowledge into the kind of competitive weapon that redefines industries – and its leaders. For this very reason, IT will continue to play an important role in our personal lives and in the companies that employ us. Those who recognize the importance of good management, not spending levels, will ultimately reap the rewards.

Tom Pisello, *CEO and Founder, Alinean Corporation, Orlando, Florida*

Letter from Roy L. Pike

Everyone will agree with Nicholas Carr that the storage, transmission, and processing of digital information has become a utility service. We outsourced our global enterprise software data center in 1998. The problem is that since most executives think of IT in much broader terms, many readers may be misled unless they read the definition of IT he provides in the footnote.

In its broadest context, information technology is all about productivity. And nothing can be more strategic right now for manufacturing and service industries than improving productivity. During the 1980s and 1990s, IT gave rise to huge improvements in productivity by changing the way individuals work– providing direct access to information and eliminating hordes of information gatherers and intermediaries who added no value to their businesses.

What Carr misses completely is that, after having improved the productivity of individual workers, IT still has the potential to improve productivity dramatically, this time by changing the way businesses work together. The new strategic task for IT is all about creating integrated business relationships in which suppliers, producers, and customers act as if they were in one company, sharing information on inventories, production, demand forecasts, lead times, and maybe costs and pricing. For decades, the solution to supply chain inefficiencies was inventory. Today, inventory is the problem. The savings in material inventories and streamlined delivery that IT can deliver will dwarf the efficiencies that have already been achieved.

Linking intercompany business processes is not using IT as a utility. A few standards have emerged in some industries, but there are practically no interindustry standards. By linking business processes, IT is and will remain of strategic importance for the next ten years.

Roy L. Pike, *Vice President of Information Technology and CIO, Millennium Chemicals, Hunt Valley, Maryland*

Letter from Vijay Gurbaxani

Nicholas Carr's article makes many of the same points that Max Hopper made in HBR in 1990. In "Rattling SABRE – New Ways to Compete on Information" (May–June), he also argued that computing was becoming a utility. So these arguments aren't new. Nevertheless, while many of Carr's arguments are sound, the situation is subtler than he would like us to believe.

The scarce resource never was technology, as Carr assumes; it was always the set of managerial capabilities needed to create value with that technology. These capabilities involve more than just managing the technology itself. They also encompass the ability to understand how investments in organizational capital complement and magnify the payoffs from technology and the ability to produce relevant information from the systems through sophisticated decision-making techniques. Recent research has demonstrated that companies spend five or ten times as much on management practices that accompany technology introductions as they do on the technology itself. What's more, as technology evolves and becomes increasingly complex, these management skills become ever scarcer.

Most companies struggle to implement a sophisticated information-based strategy. One has only to read two other articles in the May 2003 HBR – Gary Loveman's insightful "Diamonds in the Data Mine," which describes how Harrah's mined its customer information to dramatically improve its performance, and Eric Bonabeau's "Don't Trust Your Gut," which demonstrates the value of sophisticated decision-support tools–to understand why so much of what companies can do with information technology will never be found in a standard software package and why some companies will pull it off while others won't.

Carr argues that companies don't need to develop their own technology management capabilities: They can just buy computing services that embody best practices. But that assumes, first of all, that such utilities exist. Check out the current utility-computing models of the technology service providers – they are a long way from being utilities.

And when they are developed, the economics of software dictates that such shared systems must focus on a common denominator so they can be widely used. These common systems will not fit a company's processes out of the box; the firm will either need to customize the systems or change its business processes to accommodate the software. Neither approach is straightforward or always desirable. And as anyone who uses software knows, software is far from ideal.

What's more, even if companies share infrastructure and common application systems, they will not necessarily end up with identical systems or use them in similar ways. Executives will face a multitude of choices as to how they want to structure their databases and applications, what data they will collect, what information will flow out of their systems, and how they will manage it.

Still, I agree with Carr that the move to a common infrastructure is inevitable, though it will take a lot longer than he implies. Wal-Mart refuses to join industry exchanges because it believes its supply chain practices are unparalleled. And look how long it has been taking General Motors, DaimlerChrysler, and Ford to build their business-to-business exchange, Covisint, to provide the shared infrastructure and systems that will facilitate trade in the automobile industry. After investing billions of dollars, the exchange has gained only limited traction; the technological challenges and organizational changes needed are massive.

But the fundamental point is this: The move to a common infrastructure does not reduce the opportunities for competitive advantage; it increases them. Using these shared platforms, all firms will have the opportunity to build customized applications that exploit complex technological capabilities to give rise to new business strategies. When much of our investment in technology goes into shared infrastructure, the investments that we make in customization will be much more valuable.

Vijay Gurbaxani, *Faculty Chair, Professor of Information Systems, Director of the Center for Research on IT and Organizations, Graduate School of Management, University of California, Irvine*

Letter from Steven Alter

The argument in "IT Doesn't Matter" goes roughly like this: Kidneys don't matter. Kidneys are basically a commodity. Just about everyone has kidneys. People with one kidney often lead full lives with no problems. There is no evidence that CEOs with superior kidneys are more successful than CEOs with average kidneys. In fact, CEOs who spend more on their kidneys often don't do as well.

The title "IT Doesn't Matter" conveys a fallacy. An accurate but less catchy title would have been "IT Is Not the Headline." In my executive MBA courses on information systems, I use a similarly mistitled HBR case study to demonstrate why IT is essential but is not the headline. The 1997 case "The IT System That Couldn't Deliver" concerns management lapses in developing a new laptop-based tool for life insurance salespeople. The students read the case study before class and e-mail me a brief statement identifying "the system" and describing what it produces and how well it operates. Their answers are typically all over the map. As the discussion unfolds, it becomes clear that "the system" is neither the software itself nor the information system being created. Rather, it is a work system of selling insurance that has not been improved as hoped. The students usually realize that the mistakes in the case might not have happened if the CEO, CFO, and CIO had understood that the headline was the new work system, not the information system.

Still, while IT is not the headline, it certainly matters (just like kidneys) because the work systems cannot operate without IT.

Steven Alter, *Professor of Information Systems, University of San Francisco School of Business and Management, San Francisco,* *alter@usfca.edu*

Letter from Cathy Hyatt

If Nicholas Carr's article were correct, every CEO would get the same answer to the question "What is the cheapest IT solution?" Just as with electricity, companies' needs would vary only in quantity, not quality. However, those of us who have spent our careers in IT know that the answer to this question is always," It depends."

And what it depends on, more than anything else, is the company's strategy. Typically, competitive strategy leans toward one of two forms: being the low-cost provider of a commodity product or service, or being a value-added provider of a differentiated product or service. Because of the variety and complexity of IT, there is a vast number of "correct" IT solutions and investment strategies for either of these approaches – but the set of solutions that works for one will not be the same as the set that works for the other. This, I think, makes IT management, which includes the selection, maintenance, and deployment of new and ongoing IT capability, a key strategic issue.

Carr says the main problem with IT management is overspending. If only those IT managers would get together and put pressure on their vendors, he says, this could be controlled. But he misses an important point related to the strategic use of IT. Let's say a business wants a particular new IT capability that would dramatically boost its differentiation or cost advantage. If the new product or service is incompatible with the outdated hardware and software that IT management has frugally kept in service past its vendor-supported life cycle, the firm will lose out on a key strategic advantage. Those of us who have experienced this problem know that a company's hardware and software can be intricately intertwined; sometimes a single piece of outdated software can derail the deployment of important new functionality with real strategic value.

Finally, Carr's analogy comparing the ubiquity of IT with that of electricity is only effective up to a point. The complexity and variety of IT, its evolving standards in many important areas, and its incredible innovation argue against his premise that its ubiquity eliminates its strategic value. IT's history of innovation undermines his assertion that technology-related business transformations are complete. The fact that IT spending does not correlate with financial success may be related to this, as effective business-process changes are frequently made after the initial deployment of technology. An example might be a business where CRM software delivers real advantage over a competitor that, although equally able to purchase the same package, is unable to successfully deploy or use it.

To improve the business results gained from IT, corporate leaders must continue to increase its alignment with strategy. To do this, most will need to gain a greater understanding of IT, better integrate IT leadership into their strategic planning processes, and insist on greater and greater strategic and leadership capability from their IT professionals. Getting IT "right" is a difficult problem that many executives face, and while some will appreciate the silver bullet Carr offers, most, I expect, will find his naïveté discouraging.

Cathy Hyatt, *IT Consultant, San Francisco*

Letter from Chris Schlueter Langdon

I am an information systems strategy professor, so it would be expected that I would disagree with Nicholas Carr's provocative assertion that IT doesn't matter. Indeed, I do. While I agree with much of Carr's excellent – but incomplete –analysis, I disagree with his conclusion.

Certain areas in IT have become commoditized and continue to be commoditized. Just like the phone system: A business user does not have to be a network engineer to use it; the phone is a plug-and- play utility available to anyone. The same is basically true for office productivity software and computer networks – although many would argue that it is still much easier to plug in a new phone or fax machine than it is to hook up a PC to the Internet at home or to share a printer.

The analogy with the phone system breaks down at the point where Carr's analysis stops. Information systems, and software applications in particular, differ in versatility and adaptability. To exaggerate somewhat – but only a little – anything is possible with software, if not today, then tomorrow.

Increasingly, value added is being shifted from mechanical systems and their operations into software. For instance, much of the value added in the phone system is being provided by voice-over-IP software. The history of modern production is intimately tied to the automation of business processes. First, companies used steam engines, then conveyor belts, and today we use information systems, and especially software, to automate business activities. We might call it "softwarization." Companies in many industries now use ERP and CRM software to automate back-office and customer-related activities. And this softwarization is not a one-step affair, like flipping a switch, but an ongoing process. Value added is constantly being shifted into or embedded in software, with mature areas obviously becoming commoditized. Examples include computerized antilock brakes, credit cards and calling cards, airline ticketing, and yield-management systems.

Why would this process stop? Why would there suddenly be only mature areas? Are there not enough business activities left to be automated? Would it be too difficult or expensive to automate the remaining ones? The very commoditization of mature infrastructure technology reduces unit cost, which in turn frees up funding for continued softwarization without necessarily increasing total IT budgets.

Two trends ensure that the sky is the limit for softwarization. Carr mentioned the popular one –Moore's Law, which establishes that hardware will become more powerful and cheaper over time. Even more important are advances in how increased processing power can be used – which leads us into the world of systems and software architecture design, with its fast-growing jungle of acronyms and ideas. One key advance in this field has been the recent breakthrough of object-oriented programming. The concept and some tools, such as the Smalltalk programming language, have been around for decades, but only very recently has the concept been turned into commercially viable implementations.

The bottom line is that powerful hardware combined with more flexible software will continue to fuel a process in which value added is increasingly achieved with information systems. While mature areas do indeed get commoditized and probably outsourced, new softwarization should receive more, not less, of top management's attention. Why? As Michael Porter argues, "[Business] activities are the basic unit of competitive advantage." As these activities get automated using software, top management's attention should shift to information systems architecture design.

Chris Schlueter Langdon, *Assistant Professor of Information and Operations Management, Marshall School of Business, University of Southern California, Los Angeles*

Reply from Nicholas G. Carr

First and most important, let me thank these correspondents (and the many others I've heard from) for taking the time to so clearly and thoroughly express their points of view. Whatever the broader merits of my article, it has at least succeeded in setting off an important and long overdue debate about the role of information technology in business. That debate can only be constructive.

Let me quickly restate the gist of my argument, which at times gets lost in the responses. As IT's core functions – data processing, storage, and transmission –have become cheaper, more standardized, and more easily replicable, their ability to serve as the basis for competitive advantage has steadily eroded. Given this continuing and indeed inexorable trend, companies would be wise to manage IT as a commodity input, seeking to achieve competitively necessary levels of IT capability at the lowest possible cost and risk.

I find nothing in these letters to contradict that argument. As many of the writers point out, the way companies organize processes and use information plays a critical role in their ability to distinguish themselves from competitors. That's always been true and always will be true. But that does not mean that the information systems involved in managing processes and information are the source of the distinctiveness. It is better, I would argue, to start with the assumption that the technology is generic – that its functionality can be easily and quickly copied–and that the more tightly an advantage is tied to the technology, the more transient it will be. I would certainly be wary of following Paul Strassmann's recommendation that executives "be ready to engage in yet another IT investment cycle," as if spending more money on IT is itself a strategy. Many companies have taken that approach in the past, and most have come to regret it.

At the same time, I would disagree with Mark Lewis's suggestion that "IT never mattered." In the past, proprietary computer systems could indeed be the basis of long-lasting advantages, as the story of American Hospital Supply in my article shows. Dismissing the former strategic relevance of IT makes it too easy to ignore how IT's role in business has changed. And that can lead to strategic miscalculations. As Warren McFarlan and Richard Nolan point out, the value of being a first mover hinges on the speed with which fast followers catch up. As IT's power and presence have grown, fast followers have been able to catch up – or spring ahead – ever more quickly. Given the high cost of being an early investor in new IT functionality, a first mover strategy becomes harder to justify. Just because we continue to see new innovations in IT does not mean that it pays to be a pioneer.

Finally, I want to say that Jason Hittleman is right to chide me for suggesting that rigorous cost control and risk management are "boring." I used the term as a contrast to what John Seely Brown and John Hagel call "big bang" thinking in IT management – the "IT changes everything" school of thought that distorted so many business decisions during the 1990s. It was, however, an unfortunate word choice, and I apologize to the many dedicated IT professionals whose hard and valuable work is leading to a more efficient and pragmatic use of information systems – and to a more realistic understanding of those systems' limitations.

Nicholas G. Carr

ISBN 1-4120-7289-1